What Everyo... ...en WillMaker...

"By far the most comprehensive program we reviewed, offering guidance on everything...."

—USA Today

"The most complete of the five products we tried."

—The Wall Street Journal

"From a group of tough critics, Nolo's WillMaker *got the most praise... superior on every front."*

—Kiplinger's Personal Finance Magazine

*"*WillMaker *is such an easy-to-use program that users may never need to look at the manual—refreshingly painless."*

—Fortune

"The most ... comprehensive and widely praised of the will writing programs."

—Chicago Tribune

"You can complete the documents fairly quickly, or you can spend a great deal o... time exploring all the clearly written definitions and explanations...."

—PC World

"Even if you know you should see a lawyer ... Quicken's question-and-answer technique can help you sort through the options."

—BusinessWeek

"The most sophisticated legal software on the market."

—Worth

"The level of detail and complexity anticipated by the program makes WillMaker *one of the leading legal-advice programs on the market."*

—Inc.

Keep Up With the Latest in the Law and in This Product

Use Quicken WillMaker's easy Web Update feature to download the latest legal and software updates (requires Internet access). For plain-English legal information on a broad array of estate planning and personal matters, check out www.nolo.com.

Product support (including Web Update) for Quicken WillMaker 2010 ends on **January 1, 2011**. Be sure to register your product to qualify for special upgrade pricing.

Please note that legal documents created and signed before January 1, 2010 will remain legally valid and enforceable if you have used Web Update regularly. You will need to upgrade your software only if you want to create new documents or update existing documents.

An Important Message to Our Readers

This product is not a substitute for legal advice from an attorney. We've done our best to give you useful, accurate legal information, but that's not the same as personalized legal advice. If you want help understanding how the law applies to your particular circumstances, or deciding which estate planning documents are best for you and your family, you should consider seeing a qualified attorney. Estate planning documents are not valid in Louisiana.

Quicken

WillMaker 2010

BOOK & SOFTWARE KIT

SIXTH EDITION   OCTOBER 2009

Editors   SHAE IRVING
              BETSY SIMMONS

Users' Manual ELLEN BITTER
              KAREN OHLSON

Proofreading ROBERT WELLS

Index   BAYSIDE INDEXING

Priting   DELTA PRINTING SOLUTIONS, INC.

ISBN-13: 978-1-4133-1073-3 (pbk.)

ISBN-10: 1-4133-1073-7 (pbk.)

Library of Congress Cataloging-in-Publication Data to come.

Contributors

Steve Elias received his law degree from Hastings College of the Law in 1969. He worked in California, New York and Vermont as a legal aid lawyer, and in Vermont as a public defender. Steve has written and edited Nolo books on a wide range of topics, including wills, special-needs trusts, criminal law, legal research, patents, trademarks, bankruptcy and, most recently, foreclosures. Steve lives in Lakeport, California, where he provides legal advice to people doing their own bankruptcies and cohosts several radio programs with his wife on community radio station KPFZ 88.1 FM.

Shae Irving has been a Nolo author and editor since 1994, specializing in estate planning and family law issues. She has written or cowritten books and software, including *Prenuptial Agreements: How to Write a Fair and Lasting Contract; Living Wills and Powers of Attorney for California* and *Get It Together: Organize Your Records So Your Family Won't Have To.* Shae is the managing editor of Quicken WillMaker Plus and the primary author of the program's durable power of attorney for finances. Shae graduated from Berkeley Law (Boalt Hall School of Law) at the University of California, Berkeley, and briefly practiced law at a large San Francisco firm before joining Nolo's editorial staff.

Mary Randolph is Nolo VP for Editorial and Production. She earned her law degree from Berkeley Law (Boalt Hall School of Law) at the University of California. In addition working on much of the material in Quicken WillMaker Plus, she has written several books for Nolo, including *The Executor's Guide: Settling Your Loved One's Estate or Trust; 8 Ways to Avoid Probate; Every Dog's Legal Guide: A Must-Have Book for Your Owner* and *Deeds for California Real Estate.* She lives in the San Francisco Bay Area with her family.

Betsy Simmons received her law degree from Golden Gate University School of Law and is now a legal editor at Nolo specializing in estate planning. She edits the Quicken WillMaker Plus will and keeps many of the program's smaller forms up to date. Betsy also edits many popular Nolo titles, including *Plan Your Estate; Make Your Own Living Trust* and *How to Probate an Estate in California.* When Betsy's not at work she enjoys playing soccer and spending time with her family.

Ralph "Jake" Warner founded Nolo with Ed Sherman in 1972. When personal computers came along, he became a pioneer of self-help legal software, cocreating the first version of WillMaker in the early 1980s. In addition to running Nolo for much of the past three decades, Warner has been an active editor and author. He has written many books, including *Get a Life: You Don't Need a Million to Retire Well* and *How to Run a Thriving Business*. Today, he serves as chief executive officer as well as chairman of Nolo's board of directors. Warner holds a law degree from Berkeley Law (Boalt Hall School of Law) at the University of California and an undergraduate degree from Princeton.

Table of Contents

Users' Manual Table of Contents

Part 4   Reviewing, Changing and Printing Your Documents

Part 5   Managing Your Documents in Portfolios

Part 6   Managing Your Contact Information

Your Legal Companion for Estate Planning

If you're like a lot of people, you have a nagging feeling that you need to make a will—but you haven't gotten around to it because it sounds hard or expensive or just unpleasant. (Or maybe you picked up this software because you are the rare individual who loves to plan and get organized. We encourage those tendencies.) We're here to help. With Quicken WillMaker, making a legal will doesn't have to be difficult. In fact, you can probably get it done in under an hour.

You're smart to pay attention to that nagging feeling: Almost everyone needs a will. It lets you leave your property, name a guardian for young children and eliminate uncertainty about your wishes—all of which will spare your family headaches later.

Our carefully designed question-and-answer format makes the process as easy as it can be. Our goal is to help you over any hurdles by providing clear guidance and encouragement at every step.

If you're not sure how to answer a particular question, you'll find lots of practical and legal information within easy reach. Our onscreen help is there to guide you through questions large and small. (You'll probably be able to use Quicken WillMaker to make your own will, without hiring a lawyer. But we'll always alert you to situations where you might benefit from help from a lawyer or other expert.) When you're done making your will, we'll tell you everything you need to know about how to finalize it and make it legal.

You may also want to use Quicken WillMaker to leave important information to your loved ones. Our Information for Caregivers and Survivors form (included in this software) is a guide to the details of your life, from information about your bank accounts to people you'd like contacted in the event of your illness or death.

To prepare this form, the program will walk you through the particulars of your life, asking you to provide details on many topics, including things your loved ones may not know—such as the names of your doctors or whether you have life insurance. The result of this interview will be a document that will greatly aid those who need to care for you or manage your estate.

This book also provides a chapter that explains when you might want more than a will. For example you may want to use additional estate planning tools to avoid probate or reduce your estate taxes.

In the final chapter, we provide you with valuable information about how to get more help, if you need it. For example, if you have a specific question about your state's law or a complex tax question, you may want to seek out a local expert to ensure that you make the wisest choices.

Congratulations on starting your estate planning—it's a wonderful thing to do for your loved ones. We know from long experience that putting a sound estate plan into place can bring peace and satisfaction to those who take the time to do it.

About Wills

Making a will is an excellent way to ensure that your plans for leaving property to family, friends and organizations of your choice are carried out after you die. If you don't use a will or some other legal method to transfer your property when you die, state law determines what happens to your possessions. (See "Dying Without a Will," below.)

In addition to specifying who will inherit your property, you can use your will to:

- name alternates, in case your first choices die before you do
- choose someone you trust to oversee the distribution of your property after your death
- name a guardian to raise your young children if you can't, and
- name a trusted adult to manage the property that a child or young adult inherits from you. (We give you several ways to handle this; they're explained in Chapter 6.)

You can efficiently and safely write your own legal will using Quicken WillMaker. But before you start, it is a good idea to read this chapter and Chapter 2, which explain generally how wills work and how you can use Quicken WillMaker to meet your needs.

Property That Doesn't Pass Through a Will

Usually, you can't use a will to leave certain kinds of assets, including:

- property you leave through a living trust
- bank accounts for which you have named a pay-on-death beneficiary
- stocks and bonds for which you have named a transfer-on-death beneficiary
- real estate left through a transfer-on-death deed
- property owned as "community property with right of survivorship," which automatically goes to the survivor when one co-owner dies
- property owned in joint tenancy or tenancy by the entirety, which automatically goes to the surviving owners at your death, and
- individual retirement accounts (IRAs and 401(k) plans) and certain pension funds, which go to the beneficiaries you name on forms provided by the account custodian.

Legal Requirements

For a will to be legally valid, both you—the person making the will—and the will itself must meet some technical requirements.

Who Can Make a Will

Before you start your computer and get the Quicken WillMaker program going, make sure you qualify to make a will in the eyes of the law.

Age

To make a will, you must either be:

- at least 18 years old, or
- living in a state that permits people under 18 to make a will if they are married, in the military or otherwise considered legally emancipated.

Mental Competence

You must be of sound mind to prepare a valid will. While this sounds like a subjective standard, the laws generally require that you must:

- know what a will is, what it does and that you are making one
- understand the relationship between you and the people who would normally be provided for in your will, such as a spouse or children
- understand the kind and quantity of property you own, and
- be able to decide how to distribute your belongings.

This threshold of mental competence is not hard to meet. Very few wills are successfully challenged based on the charge that the person making the will was mentally incompetent. It is not enough to show that the person was forgetful or absentminded.

To have a probate court declare a will invalid usually requires proving that the testator was totally overtaken by the fraud or undue influence of another person—and that person then benefited from the wrongdoing by becoming entitled to a large amount of money or property under the will.

Interestingly, the great majority of undue influence contests are filed against attorneys who draw up wills in which they are named to take clients' property. If the person making the will was very old, ill or suffering from dementia when he or she made the will, it is obviously easier to convince a judge that undue influence occurred.

> **SEE AN EXPERT**
>
> **If a contest seems possible.** If you have any serious doubts about your ability to meet the legal requirements for making a will, or you believe your will is likely to be contested by another person for any reason, consult an experienced lawyer. (See Chapter 13.)

Will Requirements

State law determines whether a will made by a resident of the state is valid. And a will that is valid in the state where it is made is valid in all other states.

Contrary to what many people believe, a will need not be notarized to be legally valid. But adding a notarized document to the will verifying that the will was signed and witnessed can be helpful when it comes time to file the will in probate court. This option is available in all but a handful of states. (See "The Self-Proving Option" in Chapter 9.)

There are surprisingly few legal restrictions and requirements in the will-making process. In most states, a will must:

- include at least one substantive provision—either giving away some property or naming a guardian to care for minor children who are left without parents
- be signed and dated by the person making it
- be witnessed by at least two other people who are not named to take property under the will, and
- be clear enough so that others can understand what the testator intended. Nonsensical, legalistic language such as: "I hereby give, bequeath and devise" is both unwise and unnecessary.

Handwritten and Oral Wills

In about half the states, unwitnessed, handwritten wills—called holographic wills—are legally valid. And a few states accept oral wills under very limited circumstances, such as when a mortally wounded soldier utters last wishes.

But handwritten wills are fraught with possible legal problems. Most obviously, after your death, it may be difficult to prove that your unwitnessed, handwritten document was actually written by you and that you intended it to be your will. And it may be almost impossible to prove the authenticity of an oral will.

A properly signed, witnessed will is much less vulnerable to challenge by anyone claiming it was forged or fabricated. If need be, witnesses can later testify in court that the person whose name is on the will is the same person who signed it, and that making the will was a voluntary and knowing act.

Dying Without a Will

If you die without a valid will, money and other property you own at death will be divided and distributed to others according to your state's intestate succession laws. These laws divide all property among the relatives who are considered closest to you according to a set formula—and completely exclude friends and charities.

These legal formulas often do not mirror people's wishes. For example, dividing property according to intestate succession laws is often unsatisfactory if you are married and have no children, because most state laws require your spouse to share your property with your parents. The situation is even worse for unmarried couples. Except in a few states, unmarried partners receive nothing. And even in the states that offer exceptions, benefits aren't automatic—eligible couples must register their partnerships with the state.

Also, if you have minor children, another important reason to make a will is to name a personal guardian to care for them. This is an important concern of most parents, who worry that their children will be left without a caretaker if both parents die. Intestate succession laws do not deal with the issue of who will take care of your children. When you don't name a guardian in your will, it is left up to the courts and social service agencies to find and appoint a personal guardian.

Making Basic Decisions About Your Will

Making a will is not difficult, but it is undeniably a serious and sobering process. Before you begin, get organized and focus on these important questions:

- What do you own? (See Chapter 4.)
- Who should get your property? (See Chapter 5.)
- If you have minor children, who is the best person to care for them, and who is best suited to manage property you leave them? (See Chapter 3 and Chapter 6.)
- Who will see that your property is distributed according to your wishes after your death? (See Chapter 7.)

This manual offers guidance on how to use Quicken WillMaker to give legal effect to your decisions in all of these areas. The ultimate choices, however, are up to you.

Other Ways to Leave Property

A will is not the only way—and in some cases not the best way—to transfer ownership of your property when you die. Especially if you are older and own a fair amount of property, you should consider whether it makes sense to plan now to help your inheritors avoid time-consuming and expensive probate court proceedings after your death. If you have a very large estate, you may also have to think about avoiding federal or state estate tax. To learn more about using a will as part of a larger estate plan, see Chapter 12.

Making Your Own Will

As a way to decide who gets your property, the will has been around in substantially the same form for about 500 years. For the first 450 years, self-help was the rule and lawyer assistance the exception. When this country was founded, and even during the Civil War, it was highly unusual for a person to hire a lawyer to formally set out what should be done with his or her property. However, in the past 50 years, the legal profession has scored a public relations coup by convincing many people that writing a will without a lawyer is like doing your own brain surgery.

In truth, the hardest part of making a will is figuring out what property you own and who will get it when you die—questions you can answer best. Our will-making program, which has been in wide and successful use for two decades, prompts you to answer the right questions—and produces a will that fits your circumstances and is legal in your state.

But you may have a question about your particular situation that Quicken WillMaker does not answer. Or perhaps you have a very large estate and want to engage in some sophisticated tax planning. Or you may simply be comforted by having a lawyer give your Quicken WillMaker will a once-over. Whenever you have concerns such as these or simply feel that you are in over your head, it may be wise to consult an attorney with knowledge and experience in wills and estate planning. (See Chapter 13.)

Helping Someone Else Make a Will

You can use Quicken WillMaker to help a loved one or friend make a will. But you must be sure that your role is only to type in the will maker's wishes. In other words, the will maker, not you, must decide on the terms of the will. If your role exceeds these limits, a court could declare the will invalid—and you may even face legal charges.

If you decide to help someone else prepare a will, you may want to take an extra step to document your role: Make an audio or video recording of the process or ask someone else to be present as a witness while you follow the will maker's directions.

> **EXAMPLE:** Betty asks her neighbor, James, to help her make her will because her hands shake too badly to type her responses into the program. She dictates her answers to James and he types them in at her direction. She also tells James to print out the document for her to sign. For extra security, Betty's friend Wendy watches as a witness so she can later testify to James's role, if necessary.

If the person you want to help cannot clearly direct the will-making process, or if you have any concern that the person may not fully understand what it means to make a will, see an experienced estate planning attorney for help.

Other Must-Have Documents

Preparing a basic will, like the one you make with this program, is the essential first step in planning any estate. However, almost everyone should make the following basic documents, as well:

- a durable power of attorney for finances, and
- health care directives (a living will and durable power of attorney for health care).

Durable power of attorney for finances. Using this document, you name someone to take care of your finances if you are no longer able to do so. The person you choose can pay your bills, make bank deposits, handle insurance and benefits paperwork and deal with any other matters that arise—from property repairs to managing investments to taking care of a small business, if necessary.

Health care directives. These documents describe your health care wishes and name a trusted person to oversee them. (Depending on where you live, you may need one or two documents to take care of these matters. In states that offer a single document, it's often called an advance directive for health care. Other states provide two documents—frequently called a living will and a durable power of attorney for health care.) No matter what your documents are called, it's vitally important that you prepare them. Those close to you should understand the kind of medical treatment you would—or would not—want if you were unable to speak for yourself. The person you name to oversee your health care wishes can also make other necessary health care decisions for you if you are too ill or injured to direct your own care.

You can learn more about durable powers of attorney for finances and health care directives by visiting Nolo's website: www.nolo.com.

To make a durable power of attorney or a health care directive, upgrade to Quicken WillMaker Plus, which includes those two documents and many other useful forms. You can buy Quicken WillMaker Plus at www.nolo.com.

About Quicken WillMaker Wills

B ecause wills reflect how people want to leave their property, they can be as complex and intricate as life. While state laws broadly regulate the procedures for valid will making, you are generally free to write a will to meet your needs. This freedom may seem overwhelming if you are not used to wading through legal documents.

Quicken WillMaker offers considerable help. The program works by asking you to systematically answer questions. As you will soon see, you either already have enough information to answer them easily, or you can quickly get it.

> **CAUTION**
>
> **Keeping track of important information.** As you prepare to make your will, you may wish to make a list of financial and estate planning advisers you have consulted in the past. It may also be a good time to organize other estate planning documents—such as your living trust documents or life insurance policy—and to record their locations so that others will know where to find them.
>
> With Quicken WillMaker you can make an Information for Caregivers and Survivors form to help with this task. With this document, you can provide a comprehensive guide to the details of your life—ranging from information about your property and your financial accounts to the names and addresses of people you want contacted in the event of your death—for people who will care for you if you ever become incapacitated and those who will wind up your affairs after death. To find out more, click on the Document List button and select Information for Caregivers and Survivors from the list.

What You Can Do With a Quicken WillMaker Will

This chapter gives you a quick survey of what you can and cannot do with the Quicken WillMaker will. Each topic is discussed in greater detail, both in the help screens that run with the program and in other chapters in the manual.

Tailor Your Will to Your Needs

Quicken WillMaker provides you with unique guidance and options based on the state in which you live, your marital status, whether you have children and whether your children are minors. Recognizing that some people have very simple wishes for leaving their property while those of others are more complex, Quicken WillMaker lets you choose from among several approaches designed to meet your needs. For instance, if you are married, you may choose to:

- leave all property to your spouse
- leave most property to your spouse, with several specific property items going to people you name, or
- divide property among many different people and organizations. (See Chapter 5.)

Name Beneficiaries to Get Specific Property

Quicken WillMaker lets you make an unlimited number of separate gifts—called specific bequests—of cash, personal property or real estate. You may choose to leave these bequests to your spouse, children, grandchildren or anyone else—including friends, business associates, charities or other organizations. You can also use your will to leave property to a living trust, if you've established one. (See Chapter 5.)

> **EXAMPLE:** Using Quicken WillMaker, Marcia leaves her interest in the family home to her spouse Duane, her valuable coin collection to one of her children, her boat to another child, her computer to a charity and $5,000 to her two aunts, in equal shares.

> **EXAMPLE:** Raymond, a lifelong bachelor, follows Quicken WillMaker's directions and leaves his house to his favorite charity. He divides his personal possessions among 15 different relatives and friends.

EXAMPLE: Darryl and Floyd have lived together for several years. Darryl wants to leave Floyd all of his property, which includes his car, time-share ownership in a condominium, a savings account and miscellaneous personal belongings. He can use Quicken WillMaker to accomplish this.

Name Someone to Take All Remaining Property

If you have chosen an approach that lets you divide your property by making specific bequests, Quicken WillMaker also allows you to name people or organizations to take whatever property is left over after you have made the specific bequests. This property is called your residuary estate. (See "Naming Residuary Beneficiaries" in Chapter 5.)

EXAMPLE: Annie wants to make a number of small bequests to friends and charities but to leave the bulk of her property to her friend Maureen. She accomplishes this by using specific bequests to make the small gifts, and then names Maureen as residuary beneficiary. There is no need for her to list the property that goes to Maureen. The very nature of the residuary estate is that the residuary beneficiary—in this case, Maureen—gets everything that is left over after the specific bequests are distributed.

Name Alternate Beneficiaries

Using Quicken WillMaker, all beneficiaries you name take the property you leave them under your will only if they survive you by 45 days. The reason that Quicken WillMaker imposes this 45-day rule is that you do not want to leave your property to a beneficiary who dies very shortly after you do, because that property will then be passed along to that person's inheritors. These beneficiaries are not likely to be the ones you would choose to receive your property.

To account for the possibility that your first choices of beneficiaries will not meet the survivorship requirement, Quicken WillMaker allows you to name alternate beneficiaries for each of your bequests. (See Chapter 5.)

Name a Guardian to Care for Your Children

You may use Quicken WillMaker to name a personal guardian—either an individual or a couple—to care for your minor children until they reach age 18, in case there is no other legal parent to handle these duties. You may name the same guardian for all your children, or different guardians for different children. (It is important, however, that both parents name the same person or couple as guardian for any particular child; see the example below.) You will also have the opportunity to explain your choices in your will.

If your children need a guardian after your death, a court will formally review your choice. Your choice will normally be approved unless the person or couple you name refuses to assume the responsibility or the court becomes convinced that the best interests of your children would be better served if they were left in the care of someone else. (See "Your Children" in Chapter 3.)

> **EXAMPLE:** Millicent names her friend Vera to serve as personal guardian in the event that her husband, Frank, dies at the same time she does or is otherwise unavailable to care for their three children. Millicent and Frank die together in an accident. The court appoints Vera as personal guardian for all three children, since her ability to care for them has not been questioned.
>
> If Frank had written a will naming another person to serve as guardian, however, the court would have to choose between those nominated. For this reason, parents should choose the same people as personal guardians, if that is possible.

Avoiding Legalese: Per Stirpes and Per Capita

"Per stirpes" and "per capita" are legal jargon for the way children inherit property in place of a deceased parent—for example, one of these terms might govern how a granddaughter would inherit property left to her mother under a will, if her mother died before the will maker. It's not necessary for your will to include these terms. In fact, it's better to avoid them, because they can be interpreted in different ways. Instead, your Quicken WillMaker will lets you set out exactly whom you want to inherit your property, who will take the property if your first choice beneficiary doesn't survive you and the shares that they will inherit.

Name a Manager for Children's Property

Property left to minors—especially cash or other liquid assets—will usually have to be managed by an adult until the minors turn 18. In many cases, it may be most prudent to have an adult manage property left to minors until they are even older.

Property management involves safeguarding and spending the property for the young person's education, health care and basic living needs; keeping good records of these expenditures; and seeing that income taxes are paid.

Quicken WillMaker allows you to name a trusted person—or, if no one is available, you can name an institution such as a bank or trust company—to manage property left to young beneficiaries. The management methods available are different from state to state.

Quicken WillMaker also allows you to name a property guardian who will handle property that other people leave to your children or property that you leave to them outside of your will. Management ends at the age you specify in the will. What is left of the property is then distributed to the child.

Setting up property management for children is discussed in detail in Chapter 6.

> **SEE AN EXPERT**
>
> **Providing for beneficiaries with special needs.** It is common to set up management for property that will pass to a beneficiary who has a mental or physical disability, or who manages money poorly. The management provided under Quicken WillMaker is not sufficiently detailed to provide for people with disabilities or those with special problems, such as spendthrift tendencies or substance abuse. If you need this type of management, you can turn to Nolo's book, *Special Needs Trusts*, by Stephen Elias, or consult an attorney who specializes in dealing with the needs of people with disabilities. (See Chapter 13.)

Name a Caretaker for Your Pet

Many of us consider our pets to be members of the family. It's not natural to think of them as belongings that we can pass through a will. However, in the eyes of the law, pets are property. That means you can't leave money or other items directly to your pet—but you can use your will to leave your pet to a trusted caretaker. Doing so is a good way to ensure that your pet has a loving home when you die.

With Quicken WillMaker, you can name a caretaker for your pet and leave money to that person for your pet's care. If you choose to leave money to the caretaker, your document will state that you leave it "with the hope that the money will be used for the care and maintenance" of your pet. It will be up to the honor of the caretaker to use the gift as you intend. This shouldn't be a problem if you choose someone you trust to care for your pet.

You can also name an alternate in case your first-choice caretaker is not available when you die. (See "Pets" in Chapter 3.)

Cancel Debts Others Owe You

You can use Quicken WillMaker to relieve any debtors who owe you money at your death from the responsibility of paying your survivors. All you need to do is specify the debts and the people who owe them. Quicken WillMaker will then include a statement in your will canceling the debts. If a debt is canceled in this way, Quicken WillMaker also automatically wipes out any interest that has accrued on it as of your death. (See "Forgiving Debts Others Owe You" in Chapter 8.)

> **EXAMPLE:** Cynthia lent $25,000 at 10% annual interest to her son George as a down payment on a house. She uses Quicken WillMaker to cancel this debt. At Cynthia's death, George need not pay her estate the remaining balance of the loan or the interest accrued on it.

Designate How Debts, Expenses and Taxes Are Paid

Quicken WillMaker allows you to designate a particular source of money or other specific assets from which your executor should pay your debts, final expenses such as funeral and probate costs and any estate and inheritance taxes. (See Chapter 8.)

> **EXAMPLE:** Brent owns a savings account, a portfolio of stocks and bonds, an R.V. and two cars. He uses Quicken WillMaker to make a will—leaving his R.V. and stocks and bonds to his nephew, his cars to his niece and his savings account to his favorite charity, River Friends. He also designates the savings account as the source of payment of his debts and expenses of probate. Under this arrangement, River Friends will receive whatever is left in the savings account after debts and expenses of probate have been paid.

> **EXAMPLE:** Calvin's estate is valued at over $4 million. It is likely that his estate will owe some federal estate taxes when he dies. He uses Quicken WillMaker to specify that any estate tax he owes should be paid proportionately from all the property subject to the tax. If there is estate tax liability, his executor will require that each of Calvin's beneficiaries pay part of the tax in the same proportion their bequest bears to the value of Calvin's estate as a whole.

Name an Executor

With Quicken WillMaker, you can name an executor for your estate. This person or institution, called a personal representative in some states, will be responsible for making sure the provisions in your will are carried out and your property distributed as your will directs. Quicken WillMaker also produces a letter to your executor that generally explains what the job requires.

Executor or Personal Representative?		
The following states use the term "personal representative" instead of "executor," but it means the same thing. If you live in one of these states, you will see the term personal representative in your will.		
Alabama	Idaho	New Mexico
Alaska	Maine	North Dakota
Arizona	Michigan	South Carolina
Colorado	Minnesota	South Dakota
Florida	Montana	Utah
Hawaii	Nebraska	Wisconsin

The executor can be any competent adult. Commonly, people name a spouse or other close relative or friend or—for large estates or where no trusted person is able to serve—a financial institution, such as a bank or savings and loan. You are free to name two people or institutions to share the job, but doing so is often unwise. (See Chapter 7.)

It is also a good idea to use Quicken WillMaker to name an alternate executor in case your first choice becomes unable or unwilling to serve.

EXAMPLE: Rick and Phyllis both use Quicken WillMaker to complete wills naming each other as executor in case the other dies first. They both name Rick's father as an alternate executor to distribute their property in the event they die at the same time.

EXAMPLE: Pat and Babs do not wish to burden their relatives with having to take care of their fairly considerable estate. Each names the Third National Bank as executor after checking that their estate is large enough so that this bank will be willing to take the job.

What You Cannot Do With a Quicken WillMaker Will

Quicken WillMaker allows you to produce a valid and effective will designed to meet most needs. But there are some restrictions built into the program. Some of the restrictions are designed to prevent you from writing in conditions that may not be legally valid. Others are intended to keep the program simple and easy to use.

Make Bequests With Conditions

You cannot make a bequest that will take effect only if a certain condition occurs—an "if, and or but," such as "$5,000 to John if he stops smoking." Such conditional bequests are confusing and usually require someone to oversee and supervise the beneficiaries to be sure they satisfy the conditions in the will. Consider that someone would have to constantly check up on John to make sure he never took a puff—and someone would have to wrench away his property if he ever got caught in the act.

So, to use Quicken WillMaker, you must be willing to leave property to people outright; you cannot make them jump through hoops or change their behavior to get it.

CAUTION

Takers must survive by 45 days. To ensure that property goes to people you want to have it, Quicken WillMaker automatically imposes the condition that each of your beneficiaries must survive you by 45 days. If they do not survive you by that amount of time, the property you had slated for them will pass instead to the person or institution you have named as an alternate beneficiary, or it will go to the one you have named to take your residuary estate.

Write Joint Wills

In the past, it was common for a married couple who had an agreed upon scheme for how to distribute all their property to write one document together: a joint will. But time has shown that setup to be crawling with problems.

Quicken WillMaker requires that each spouse make his or her own will, even if both agree about how their property is to be distributed. This limitation is not imposed to annoy people or defeat their intentions; there is solid legal reasoning behind it.

Joint wills are intended to prevent the surviving spouse from changing his or her mind about what to do with the property after the first spouse dies. The practical effect is to tie up the property for years in title and probate determinations—often until long after the second spouse dies. Also, many court battles are fought over whether the surviving spouse is legally entitled to revoke any part of the joint will.

There are still some lawyers who will agree to write joint wills for clients, but they take the risk that such wills may become cumbersome or may even be found invalid in later court challenges. For these reasons, it is best for both spouses to write separate wills—a bit more time-consuming, perhaps, but a lot safer from a legal standpoint.

Creating Identical Wills

While you can't create a joint will using Quicken WillMaker, you can create identical wills—that is, two separate wills in which all the provisions (such as beneficiaries and children's guardians) are the same. If you want to do this, the program provides an easy shortcut. See "Creating an Identical Will for a Spouse or Partner," in the Users' Manual.

Explain the Reasons for Leaving Your Property

Most of the time, the act of leaving property to people—or choosing not to leave them anything—speaks for itself. Occasionally, however, people making wills want to explain to survivors the reasons they left property as they did. This might be the case, for example, if you opt to leave one of your two children more property than the other to compensate for the loan you made during your lifetime to help one of them buy a house. Although the desire to make such explanations is understandable, Quicken WillMaker does not allow you to do it in your will, because of the risk that you might add legally confusing language to the document.

However, there is an easy and legally safe way to provide your heirs with explanations for your bequests. You can draft a letter that you can attach to your will, explaining your reasons for leaving property to some people—or not leaving it to others. (See Chapter 11.)

Name Coguardians for Children's Property

You may name only one guardian to care for the property left to your young children. While you may choose different property guardians for different children, you may not name two people to share the responsibility. (See Chapter 6.)

At first glance, it may seem to be a good idea to divide up the job—after all, sometimes two heads are better than one. But naming more than one property guardian often presents more problems than it solves because those two people will have to make every decision together. A difference of opinion could require court intervention, which will cost both time and money. It is better to name just one trustworthy person to make decisions about your children's property, and then name a second equally trustworthy person to take over the job if the first one becomes unavailable.

In contrast, note that you may name a couple to serve as your children's *personal* guardians. A personal guardian makes decisions about the well being of the children, rather than the children's property. When those types of decisions will be made in a family setting with two adults, the ability to name a couple is important—so that either adult may take the child to the doctor or to school, for example.

CAUTION

Review wills to avoid conflicts. People who jointly own property or have children together should review their wills together to be sure they do not provide conflicting information—such as each naming two different guardians for any one child.

Control Property After Death

Property given to others in a Quicken WillMaker will must go to them as soon as you die. You cannot make a bequest by will with the property to be used for a person's life and then be given to a second person when the first person dies. Such an arrangement involves too many variables for both will makers and beneficiaries to handle. You will need to use more complex estate planning strategies to carry out this type of plan. (See Chapter 13.)

> EXAMPLE: Emory wants his grandchildren to get his house when he dies but wants his wife to have the right to live in the house until her death. Emory cannot use Quicken WillMaker to accomplish this. Emory would have to leave his house in trust to his spouse for her life and then to his grandchildren upon his spouse's death.

Require a Bond for Executors or Property Managers

A bond is like an insurance policy that protects the beneficiaries in the unlikely event that the executor wrongfully spends or distributes estate property. Because the premium or fee that must be paid for a bond comes out of the estate—leaving less money for the beneficiaries—most wills for small or moderate estates do not require one.

Following this general practice, the will produced by the Quicken WillMaker program does not require a bond. Instead, take care to appoint someone you know to be trustworthy.

Leave Property to Your Pet

Animals aren't legally permitted to own property, so you can't use your will to make gifts to your pet. If you name your pet to receive property through your will, that gift will be void and the intended gift and the pet will become part of your residuary estate.

That said, you can use your will to name a caretaker for your pet and to leave money to that person requesting that they use it for the care of your pet. (See "Pets" in Chapter 3.)

Customize a No-Contest Clause

The Quicken WillMaker will contains a standard no-contest clause. This clause states that a beneficiary who challenges your will after your death forfeits any gifts you have made to that beneficiary under your will. The property you left to the beneficiary would be distributed as if they died before you.

> **EXAMPLE:** Marah's will leaves $15,000 to her sister, Karen. Marah's nephew, Nathaniel, is the alternate beneficiary for the gift. Marah leaves the rest of her property to her partner of five years, Luke. After Marah's death, Karen challenges the will, believing that Marah intended to leave her more property and that Luke unfairly influenced Marah. Under the terms of the no-contest clause, the $15,000 gift to Karen is immediately revoked and the money passes to Nathaniel.

In reality, most states will not uphold a no-contest clause if the challenger has a good reason to object to the will—for example, if the challenger shows that the will is not valid because the signer's name was forged. Other states go further and do not uphold no-contest clauses for any reason.

Although states vary in their willingness to uphold no-contest clauses, all Quicken WillMaker wills include a standard no-contest clause for an important purpose: to discourage challenges to your will by those who do not like what you leave them. If a beneficiary challenges your will anyway, and a court decides not to enforce the no-contest clause, the rest of your will is effective as written.

If you do not want to include a no-contest clause, or if you do not like the way the clause would affect the distribution of your estate following a challenge, see an experienced estate planning lawyer for advice.

A Look at a Quicken WillMaker Will

You may find it helpful to take a look at a Quicken WillMaker will, but do not be alarmed if the sample will does not match the one you produce. Your Quicken WillMaker will is tailored to your property, circumstances and state laws. Nearly every paragraph, or clause, of the sample will is followed by an explanation.

Will of Natalie DeJarlais

Part 1. Personal Information

I, Natalie DeJarlais, a resident of the State of California, Alameda County, declare that this is my will.

Part 2. Revocation of Previous Wills

I revoke all wills and codicils that I have previously made.

This provision makes clear that this is the will to be used—not any other wills or amendments to those wills, called codicils, that were made earlier. To prevent possible confusion, all earlier wills and codicils should also be physically destroyed.

Part 3. Marital Status

I am married to Michael Sexton.

Here you identify your spouse if you are married—or your partner, if you are in a registered domestic partnership, civil union or other marriage-like relationship recognized by your state. If you are not married or in a registered partnership, this provision will not appear in your will.

Part 4. Children

I have the following children now living: Sammie DeJarlais and Chester DeJarlais.

This part of your will should list all of your natural-born and adopted children; your stepchildren should not be included here. By naming all your children, you will prevent a child from claiming that he or she was accidentally overlooked in your will. It will also ward off later claims that any child is entitled to take a share of your property against your wishes.

Part 5. Pets

I leave my Boston terrier, Clementine, and $1,500, to Ann Heron, with the hope that the money will be used for Clementine's care and maintenance. If Ann Heron does not survive me, I leave Clementine and $2,000 to Michael Sexton, with the hope that the money will be used for Clementine's care and maintenance.

> *Here you can leave your pet to a trusted caretaker. You can also leave money to the caretaker with a request that the caretaker use the money for your pet's care.*

Part 6. Disposition of Property

A beneficiary must survive me for 45 days to receive property under this will. As used in this will, the phrase "survive me" means to be alive or in existence as an organization on the 45th day after my death.

> *This language means that to receive property under your will, a person must be alive for at least 45 days after your death. Otherwise, the property will go to whomever you named as an alternate. This language permits you to choose another way to leave your property if your first choice dies within a short time after you do.*
>
> *This will clause also prevents the confusion associated with the simultaneous death of two spouses, when it is hard to tell who gets the property they have left to each other. Property left to a spouse who dies within 45 days of the first spouse, including a spouse who dies simultaneously, will go to the person or organization named as alternate.*

If I leave property to be shared by two or more beneficiaries, and any of them does not survive me, I leave his or her share to the others equally unless this will provides otherwise.

> *This clause states that if you leave a gift to two or more beneficiaries without stating the percentage each should receive, the beneficiaries will share the gift equally. This clause is included as a catchall; you can determine the shares for almost every shared gift.*

My residuary estate is all property I own at my death that is subject to this will that does not pass under a general or specific bequest, including all failed or lapsed bequests.

This definition is included so that you and your survivors are clear on the meaning of "residuary estate."

I leave $10,000 to Justin Disney. If Justin Disney does not survive me, I leave this property to Bhamita Ranchod.

This language leaves a specific item of property—$10,000—to a named beneficiary, Justin Disney. If Justin Disney does not survive the testator, then Bhamita Ranchod will get the money.

I leave my rare stamp collection to Ann Heron, Eric K. Workman and André Zivkovich in the following shares: Ann Heron shall receive a 1/4 share. Eric K. Workman shall receive a 1/4 share. André Zivkovich shall receive a 1/2 share.

This language leaves a specific item of property—a stamp collection—to three people in unequal shares.

I leave my collection of Nash cars to The Big Sky Auto Museum and Richard Jenkins in equal shares. If Richard Jenkins does not survive me, I leave his or her share of this property to Patricia Jenkins.

This will leaves specific property to an organization and a person equally. Since the testator here was concerned about providing for the possibility that the person would not survive to take the property, she named an alternate for him.

I leave my residuary estate to my spouse, Michael Sexton.

This clause gives the residuary estate—all property that does not pass under this will in specific bequests—to the testator's spouse. Your residuary estate may be defined differently depending on your plans for leaving your property.

If Michael Sexton does not survive me, I leave my residuary estate to Sammie DeJarlais and Chester DeJarlais in a children's pot trust to be administered under the children's pot trust provisions.

> *If the person named here to take the residuary estate does not survive the testator, the residuary estate will pass to the two people named: the testator's children. The property will be put in one pot for both of the children to use as they mature. Specifics of how this pot trust operates are explained later in the will. Keep in mind that, in this example, the pot trust will come into being only if the testator's spouse does not survive the testator by at least 45 days.*

If both of these children are age 18 or older at my death, my residuary estate shall be distributed to them directly in equal shares.

> *This clause makes clear what should happen if the children are older than the age at which the testator specified the pot trust should end. In this case, no pot trust will be created; the children will get the property directly and divide it evenly.*

If either of these children do not survive me, I leave his or her share to the other child.

> *This clause explains that if either child here does not survive, the other will get the property directly.*

If Michael Sexton, Sammie DeJarlais and Chester DeJarlais all do not survive me, I leave my residuary estate to Delia Holt.

All personal and real property that I leave in this will shall pass subject to any encumbrances or liens placed on the property as security for the repayment of a loan or debt.

> *This language explains that whoever gets any property under this will also gets the mortgage and other legal claims against the property, such as liens. And anyone who takes property that is subject to a loan, such as a car loan, gets the debt as well as the property.*

Part 7. Custodianship Under the Uniform Transfers to Minors Act

All property left in this will to Delia Holt shall be given to James Leung as custodian under the California Uniform Transfers to Minors Act, to be held until Delia Holt reaches age 21. If James Leung is unwilling or unable to serve as custodian of property left to Delia Holt under this will, Michael Eisenberg shall serve instead.

> *This clause provides that all property left to the child named in the clause will be managed by the person named as the custodian until the child turns the age indicated. An alternate custodian is also named in case the first-choice custodian is unable or unwilling to serve when the time comes.*

Part 8. Children's Pot Trust

A. Beneficiaries of Children's Pot Trust

Sammie DeJarlais and Chester DeJarlais shall be the beneficiaries of the children's pot trust provided for in this will. If a beneficiary survives me but dies before the children's pot trust terminates, that beneficiary's interest in the trust shall pass to the surviving beneficiaries of the children's pot trust.

B. Trustee of Children's Pot Trust

Dave Jenkins shall serve as the trustee of the children's pot trust. If Dave Jenkins is unable or unwilling to serve, Keely Jenkins shall serve instead.

C. Administration of the Children's Pot Trust

The trustee shall manage and distribute the assets in the children's pot trust in the following manner.

The trustee may distribute trust assets as he or she deems necessary for a beneficiary's health, support, maintenance and education. Education includes, but is not limited to, college, graduate, postgraduate and vocational studies and reasonably related living expenses.

In deciding whether or not to make distributions, the trustee shall consider the value of the trust assets, the relative current and future needs of each beneficiary and each beneficiary's other income, resources and sources of support. In doing so, the trustee has the discretion to make distributions that benefit some beneficiaries more than others or that completely exclude others.

Any trust income that is not distributed by the trustee shall be accumulated and added to the principal.

D. Termination of the Children's Pot Trust

When the youngest surviving beneficiary of this children's pot trust reaches 18, the trustee shall distribute the remaining trust assets to the surviving beneficiaries in equal shares.

If none of the trust beneficiaries survives to the age of 18, the trustee shall, at the death of the last surviving beneficiary, distribute the remaining trust assets to that beneficiary's estate.

Part 9. Individual Child's Trust

A. Beneficiaries and Trustees

All property left in this will to Bhamita Ranchod shall be held in a separate trust for Bhamita Ranchod until she reaches age 25. The trustee of the Bhamita Ranchod trust shall be Connor Jenkins.

> *This clause provides that all property given to the child named in the clause shall be held in trust—that is, managed strictly for the benefit of the child— by the person named as the trustee until the child turns the age indicated. An alternate trustee may also be named in case the first-choice trustee is unable or unwilling to serve when the time comes.*

B. Administration of an Individual Child's Trust

The trustee of an individual child's trust shall manage and distribute the assets in the trust in the following manner.

Until the trust beneficiary reaches the age specified for final distribution of the principal, the trustee may distribute some or all of the principal or net income of the trust as the trustee deems necessary for the child's health, support, maintenance and education. Education includes, but is not limited to, college, graduate, postgraduate and vocational studies and reasonable living expenses.

> *This clause lets the trustee spend the trust principal and income for the child's general living, health and educational needs. The clause gives the trustee great latitude in how this is done and what amount is spent.*

In deciding whether or not to make a distribution to a beneficiary, the trustee may take into account the beneficiary's other income, resources and sources of support.

> *This clause lets the trustee withhold the trust principal or income from the trust beneficiary if, in the trustee's opinion, the beneficiary has sufficient income from other sources.*

Any trust income that is not distributed by the trustee shall be accumulated and added to the principal.

> *Every trust involves two types of property: the property in the trust— called the trust principal—and the income that is earned by investing the principal. This clause assures that the trustee must add to the trust principal any income that is earned on the principal, unless the income is distributed to the trust beneficiary.*

C. Termination of an Individual Child's Trust

An individual child's trust shall terminate as soon as one of the following events occurs:

- the beneficiary reaches the age stated above, in which case the trustee shall distribute the remaining principal and accumulated net income of the trust to the beneficiary

- the beneficiary dies, in which case the principal and accumulated net income of the trust shall pass under the beneficiary's will, or if there is no will, to his or her heirs, or

- the trust principal is exhausted through distributions allowed under these provisions.

> *This clause sets out three events that may cause the trust to end. The first is when the minor or young adult reaches the age specified for the trust to end. If the trust ends for this reason, the minor or young adult gets whatever trust principal and accumulated income is left. The trust will also end if the minor or young adult dies before the age set for the trust to end. If the trust ends for this reason, the principal and income accumulated in*

the trust goes to whomever the young adult named in his or her will to get it or, if there is no will, to the minor or young adult's legal heirs—such as parents, brothers and sisters. A third occurrence that will cause the trust to end is when there is no trust principal left—or so little left that it's no longer financially feasible to maintain it.

Part 10. General Trust Administration Provisions

All trusts established in this will shall be managed subject to the following provisions.

A. Transferability of Interests

The interests of any beneficiary of all trusts established by this will shall not be transferable by voluntary or involuntary assignment or by operation of law and shall be free from the claims of creditors and from attachment, execution, bankruptcy or other legal process to the fullest extent permitted by law.

This important clause removes the trust principal and accumulated income from the reach of the minor or young adult's creditors—while it is being held in the trust. Also, this clause prevents the minor or young adult from transferring ownership of the principal or accumulated interest to others—again, while it is in the trust. Once property is distributed to the minor or young adult, however, there are no restrictions on what he or she can do with it.

B. Powers of the Trustee

In addition to other powers granted a trustee in this will, a trustee shall have the powers to:

1. Invest and reinvest trust funds in every kind of property and every kind of investment, provided that the trustee acts with the care, skill, prudence and diligence under the prevailing circumstances that a prudent person acting in a similar capacity and familiar with such matters would use.

2. Receive additional property from any source and acquire or hold properties jointly or in undivided interests or in partnership or joint venture with other people or entities.

3. Enter, continue or participate in the operation of any business, and incorporate, liquidate, reorganize or otherwise change the form or terminate the operation of the business and contribute capital or loan money to the business.

4. Exercise all the rights, powers and privileges of an owner of any securities held in the trust.

5. Borrow funds, guarantee or indemnify in the name of the trust and secure any obligation, mortgage, pledge or other security interest, and renew, extend or modify any such obligations.

6. Lease trust property for terms within or beyond the term of the trust.

7. Prosecute, defend, contest or otherwise litigate legal actions or other proceedings for the protection or benefit of the trust; pay, compromise, release, adjust or submit to arbitration any debt, claim or controversy; and insure the trust against any risk and the trustee against liability with respect to other people.

8. Pay himself or herself reasonable compensation out of trust assets for ordinary and extraordinary services, and for all services in connection with the complete or partial termination of this trust.

9. Employ and discharge professionals to aid or assist in managing the trust and compensate them from the trust assets.

10. Make distributions to the beneficiaries directly or to other people or organizations on behalf of the beneficiaries.

> *This list of powers should cover the gamut of activities that trustees might be called upon to exercise in administering any trust set up in this will.*

C. Severability

The invalidity of any trust provision of this will shall not affect the validity of the remaining trust provisions.

> *This language ensures that in the unlikely event that a court finds any individual part of this trust to be invalid, the rest of the document will remain in effect.*

Part 11. Personal Guardian

If at my death a guardian is needed to care for my children, I name Ann Heron as personal guardian. If this person is unable or unwilling to serve as personal guardian, I name Michael Eisenberg to serve instead.

Reasons for my choice for guardian for all my children: Ann Heron has established a close relationship with all of the children. She frequently takes care of them when my husband and I must work on weekends—and her training as a doctor makes her especially knowledgeable about handling their health care needs. Best of all, she is a loving and trustworthy friend who has unerring judgment and common sense—an excellent choice to raise the children if Michael and I cannot.

No personal guardian shall be required to post bond.

This clause names someone to provide parental-type care for a minor child if there is no legal (biological or adoptive) parent able to provide it. The clause also provides for an alternate to step in if the first choice is not able or willing to act when the moment comes. When making your own will, be aware that if there is another legal parent on the scene, that parent will usually be awarded custody of the children, unless a court concludes that the children would be at risk of harm. The explanation provided for the choice helps ensure that a court will follow your reasoning and approve your choice of guardian. The clause also provides that the personal guardian need not provide a bond—a kind of insurance of good performance— to guarantee faithful performance of his or her duties.

Part 12. Property Guardian

If at my death, a guardian is needed to care for any property belonging to Sammie DeJarlais or Chester DeJarlais, I name Eric K. Workman as property guardian. If Eric K. Workman is unwilling or unable to serve as property guardian, I name Justin Disney to serve instead.

No property guardian shall be required to post bond.

This clause appoints someone to manage property that passes to your children outside of your will. For example, if your children receive an inheritance from another relative, proceeds from a life insurance policy or income from a trust, and those instruments do not provide a property guardian, you can name an adult to manage those funds until the children become adults. You may also appoint an alternate property guardian in case your first choice is not able or willing to serve when the time comes. The clause also provides that the personal guardian need not provide a bondto guarantee that he or she will act faithfully.

Part 13. Forgiveness of Debts

I wish to forgive all debts specified below, plus accrued interest as of the date of my death: Sheila Jenkins, April 6, 2007, $10,000.

Forgiving a debt is equivalent to making a bequest of money. It is a common way to equalize what you leave to all your children when you have loaned one of them some money—that is, the amount that you would otherwise leave that child can be reduced by the amount of the debt being forgiven.

Part 14. Executor

I name Michael Sexton to serve as my executor. If Michael Sexton is unwilling or unable to serve as executor, I name Ann Heron to serve as my executor.

No executor shall be required to post bond.

This clause identifies the choices for executor and an alternate executor who will take over if the first choice is unable or unwilling to serve when the time comes.

Part 15. Executor's Powers

I direct my executor to take all actions legally permissible to have the probate of my will done as simply and as free of court supervision as possible under the laws of the state having jurisdiction over this will, including filing a petition in the appropriate court for the independent administration of my estate.

This clause sets out the specific authority that the executor will need to competently manage the estate until it has been distributed under the terms of the will. The will language expresses your desire that your executor work as free from court supervision as possible. This will cut down on delays and expense.

When you print out your will, a second paragraph will list a number of specific powers that your executor will have, if necessary. It also makes clear that the listing of these specific powers does not deprive your executor of any other powers that he or she has under the law of your state. The general idea is to give your executor as much power as possible, so that he or she will not have to go to court and get permission to take a particular action.

Part 16. Payment of Debts

Except for liens and encumbrances placed on property as security for the repayment of a loan or debt, I direct all debts and expenses owed by my estate to be paid using the following assets: Account #666777 at Cudahy Savings Bank.

This clause states how debts will be paid. Depending on the choice you make when using Quicken WillMaker, your debts may be paid either from specific assets you designate or from your residuary estate—all the property covered by your will that does not pass through a specific bequest.

Part 17. Payment of Taxes

I direct that all estate and inheritance taxes assessed against property in my estate or against my beneficiaries to be paid using the following assets: Account #939494050 at the Independence Bank, Central Branch.

This clause states how any estate or death taxes owed by the estate or beneficiaries should be paid. This will usually apply only to people whose estate has a net value greater than $3.5 million or more. Depending on the choice you make when operating Quicken WillMaker, your taxes may be paid from all of your property, from specific assets you designate or by your executor according to the law of your state.

Part 18. No-Contest Provision

If any beneficiary under this will contests this will or any of its provisions, any share or interest in my estate given to the contesting beneficiary under this will is revoked and shall be disposed of as if that contesting beneficiary had not survived me.

> *This harsh-sounding clause is intended to discourage anyone who receives anything under the will from challenging its legality for the purpose of receiving a larger share. Many states will not enforce a no-contest clause if the challenger has a good reason for the contest. Other states have passed laws specifically stating that a no-contest clause will not be enforced. If a court decides not to carry out the no-contest clause in your will, the rest of the document will be enforced as written.*

////
/////
/////
/////
/////
////
/////
/////
/////
/////
/////
/////
/////
/////
/////

> *These hashmarks will automatically appear to fill up the rest of the page so that your signature appears with some text of the will—one way to help guard against an unethical survivor tampering with the document.*

Part 19. Severability

If any provision of this will is held invalid, that shall not affect other provisions that can be given effect without the invalid provision.

> *This is standard language that ensures that in the unlikely event that a court finds any individual part of your will to be invalid, the rest of the document will remain in effect.*

SIGNATURE

I, Natalie DeJarlais, the testator, sign my name to this instrument, this

_____ day of _____, _____,

at _____. I declare that I sign and execute this instrument as my last will, that I sign it willingly, and that I execute it as my free and voluntary act. I declare that I am of the age of majority or otherwise legally empowered to make a will, and under no constraint or undue influence.

Signature: _____

WITNESSES

We, the witnesses, sign our names to this document, and declare that the testator willingly signed and executed this document as the testator's last will.

In the presence of the testator, and in the presence of each other, we sign this will as witnesses to the testator's signing.

To the best of our knowledge, the testator is of the age of majority or otherwise legally empowered to make a will, is mentally competent and under no constraint or undue influence. We declare under penalty of perjury that the foregoing is true and correct, this _____ day

of _____, _____ at _____

_____.

First Witness

Sign your name: _____

Print your name: _____

Address: _____

City, State: _____

Second Witness

Sign your name: _____

Print your name: _____

Address: _____

City, State: _____

About You and Yours

As you go through Quicken WillMaker, you will first be asked to answer a number of questions about yourself and your family. This chapter discusses those questions in the order in which they appear in the program.

Your Name

Enter your name—first, middle, if you choose, then last—in the same form that you use on other formal documents, such as your driver's license or bank accounts. This may or may not be the name that appears on your birth certificate.

If you customarily use more than one name for business purposes, list all of them in your Quicken WillMaker answer, separated by aka, which stands for "also known as."

There is room for you to list several names. But use your common sense. Your name is needed here to identify you and all the property you own. Be sure to include all names in which you have held bank accounts, stocks, bonds, real estate or other property. But you need not list every nickname, or names you use for nonbusiness purposes.

Your Gender

Quicken WillMaker also asks you to state whether you are male or female. This is not to be nosy, but to avoid the awkward "he or she" in your final document.

Your Social Security Number

At the end of the interview, Quicken WillMaker will give you the option to enter your nine-digit Social Security number. If you choose to enter it, the number will *not* be included in your will, where it could become part of the public record. Instead, the program will print your Social Security number in a letter for your executor that prints with your will.

...te of your legal residence, sometimes
...ate where you make your home now and
...nformation is vital for a number of will-
...ant to check your answer for accuracy.

...ship
...ptions for young beneficiaries
- now your will can be admitted into probate, and
- whether your property will be subject to state inheritance tax.

If you live in two or more states during the year and have business relationships in both, you may not be sure which state is your legal residence.

Choose the state where you are the most rooted—that is, the state in which you:

- are registered to vote
- register your motor vehicles
- own valuable property—especially property with a title document, such as a house or car
- have checking, savings and other investment accounts, and
- maintain a business.

To avoid confusion, it is best to keep all or at least most of your roots in one state, if possible. For people with larger estates, ideally this should be in a state that does not levy an inheritance tax. (See "Estate and Inheritance Taxes" in Chapter 8.)

CAUTION

Wills valid in the United States only. Quicken WillMaker produces valid wills in all of the continental United States except for Louisiana—and the program guides you by showing you screens geared specifically to the state of residence you indicate when using it.

Because the property and probate laws in Puerto Rico and Guam, for example, may differ from a state you have selected to use in making your will, we do not guarantee that a Quicken WillMaker will is valid there. However, some users who reside outside the United States do use Quicken WillMaker to help draft their wills and then have them looked over by an experienced local professional.

CAUTION

If your choice is not clear. If you do not maintain continuous ties with a particular state, or if you have homes in both the United States and another country, consult a lawyer to find out which state to list as your legal domicile when using Quicken WillMaker.

Living Overseas

If you live overseas temporarily because you are in the armed services, your residence will be the home of record you declared to the military authorities.

Normally, your home of record is the state you lived in before you received your assignment, where your parents or spouse live or where you now have a permanent home. If there is a close call between two states, consider the factors listed above for determining a legal residence or get advice from the military legal authorities.

If you live overseas for business or education, you probably still have ties with a particular state that would make it your legal residence. For example, if you were born in Wisconsin, lived there for many years, registered to vote there and receive mail there in care of your parents who still live in Milwaukee, then Wisconsin is your legal residence for purposes of making a will.

Your County

Including your county in your will is optional but recommended. Including it will help others identify you and track down your property after your death.

Also, a county name may provide those handling your estate with important direction, because wills go through probate in the court system of the county where you last resided, no matter where you died. The one exception is real estate: That property is probated in the court of the county in which it is located.

If you live in Alaska, which is divided into boroughs and judicial districts instead of counties, you may enter the name of your borough. The correct term will appear in your will.

Marital or Domestic Partnership Status

Quicken WillMaker asks you to indicate your marital or domestic partnership status. (When we say "domestic partnership," we mean any marriage-like partnership registered with a state government, including civil unions and reciprocal beneficiary relationships.) The law treats married people and registered domestic partners differently than other will makers, so your answer to this question is important. Rest assured, however, that you will be able to leave your property in almost any way you please, regardless of your relationship status.

It will probably be easy to select your relationship status. However, if you are separated, have filed for divorce or have a same-sex partner, the answer may not be clear. Read the following sections to help you make the best choice.

If you are married or in a registered domestic partnership, you should also review the property ownership laws affecting married and partnered people. (See "Property Ownership Rules for Married People" in Chapter 4.)

The Importance of Your Marital Status

You should make a new will whenever you marry or divorce. (See Chapter 10.)

If your marital status changes but your will does not, your new spouse or ex-spouse may get more or less of your property than you intend. For example, if you remarry after making a will and do not provide for the new spouse—either in the will or through transfers outside the will—your spouse, in many states, may be entitled to claim a big share of your property at your death.

Also, if you name a spouse in a will, then divorce or have the marriage annulled and die before making a new will, state laws will produce different, often unexpected, results. In most states, the former spouse will automatically get nothing. In other states, the former spouse is entitled to take the property as set out in the will.

In a few states, registered domestic partnerships provide the same rights and responsibilities as marriage. In those states, changes in your partnership status may affect the distribution of your property. Therefore, like married folks, you should make a new will whenever your domestic partnership status changes.

Divorce

If you're not sure whether or not you are legally divorced, make sure you see a copy of the final order signed by a judge. To track down a divorce order, contact the court clerk in the county where you believe the divorce occurred. You will need to give the first and last names of you and your former spouse and make a good guess at what year the divorce became final. If you cannot locate a final decree of divorce, it is safest to assume you are still legally married.

If the divorce was supposed to have taken place outside the United States, it may be difficult to verify. If you have any reason to think that someone you consider to be a former spouse might claim to be married to you at your death because an out-of-country divorce was not legal, consult a lawyer. (See Chapter 13.)

Separation

Many married couples, contemplating divorce or reconciliation, live apart from one another, sometimes for several years. Although this often feels like a murky limbo while you are living it, for will-making purposes, your status is straightforward: You are legally married until a court issues a formal decree of divorce, signed by a judge. This is true even if you and your spouse are legally separated as declared in a legal document. Note that many separation agreements, however, set out rights and restrictions that may affect your ownership of property.

Common Law Marriage

It is uncommon to have a common law marriage. In most states, common law marriage does not exist.

But in the states listed below, couples can become legally married if they live together and either hold themselves out to the public as being married or actually intend to be married to one another. Once these conditions are met, the couple is legally married. And the marriage will still be valid even if they later move to a state that does not allow couples to form common law marriages there.

No matter what state you live in, if either you or the person you live with is still legally married to some other person, you cannot have a common law marriage.

The following states recognize some form of common law marriage:
- Alabama
- Colorado
- District of Columbia
- Georgia (if created before 1/1/97)
- Idaho (if created before 1/1/96)
- Iowa
- Kansas

- Montana
- New Hampshire (for inheritance purposes only)
- Ohio (if created before 10/10/91)
- Oklahoma
- Pennsylvania (if created before 1/1/05)
- Rhode Island
- South Carolina
- Texas, and
- Utah.

In addition, a handful of states—including Florida, Indiana, Mississippi, Nebraska, Nevada, New Jersey and South Dakota—recognize common law marriages if they were created long ago. If you live in one of these states and you entered into what you believe to be a common law marriage before 1970, you may want to consult a lawyer to determine the legal status of your relationship.

There is no such thing as a common law divorce; no matter how your marriage begins, you must go through formal divorce proceedings to end it.

Same-Sex Couples

The laws affecting same-sex couples are in great flux. Most states still don't legally recognize same-sex relationships. But a handful of states permit same-sex couples to marry, while many others offer a variety of rights to lesbian and gay couples who register their relationships. (See "Same-Sex Partners and State Laws," below, for details.)

CAUTION

Federal law does not recognize same-sex partnerships. The federal government does not currently recognize any same-sex relationships, no matter what state law says. (This is because of a federal law called the Defense of Marriage Act.) So same-sex couples who marry or register their partnerships are not entitled to the federal estate and gift tax benefits married couples enjoy—or to Social Security benefits, or any of the more than 1,000 other benefits extended to heterosexual married couples.

Same-Sex Partners and State Laws	
California	Registered domestic partnerships provide the same rights married couples enjoy, including community property rights (see "Property Ownership Rules for Married People" in Chapter 4) and the right to inherit from a deceased partner who didn't make a will. From mid-June until November 2008, California allowed same-sex couples to marry. Although marriages entered into during that time are valid, same-sex couples can no longer marry. It is technically possible that you can be both married and in a domestic partnership under California law; however, to avoid confusion we ask you to choose just one status when you make your will. Doing so will not affect the way your property is distributed after your death.
Connecticut	Same-sex couples are allowed to marry. The state also offers civil unions that give partners all the rights of married couples under state law, including inheritance rights. Although it is technically possible that you can be both married and in a civil union under Connecticut law, to avoid confusion we ask you to choose one status or the other when you make your will. Doing so will not affect the way your property is distributed after your death.
District of Columbia	Registered domestic partners are given most of the rights that married couples have, including inheritance rights.
Hawaii	Allows reciprocal beneficiary relationships, giving registered partners most of the inheritance rights of married couples.
Iowa	Same-sex couples are allowed to marry.
Maine	Same-sex couples are allowed to marry beginning September 1, 2009. The state also offers domestic partnerships that give inheritance rights. Although it is technically possible that you could be both married and in a domestic partnership under Maine law, you must choose one status or the other when you make your will. If this applies to you, we recommend that you indicate that you are married because, in Maine, your marriage provides a greater number of rights than does your domestic partnership.
Massachusetts	Same-sex couples are allowed to marry.

Same-Sex Partners and State Laws (continued)

New Hampshire	Beginning January 1, 2010, New Hampshire will allow same-sex couples to marry. The state also offers civil unions that give partners all the rights of married couples under state law, including inheritance rights. Although it is technically possible that you can be both married and in a civil union under New Hampshire law, to avoid confusion we ask you to choose one status or the other when you make your will. Doing so will not affect the way your property is distributed after your death.
New Jersey	Provides for both domestic partnerships and civil unions, though you can't have both at the same time. (If you are registered as domestic partners and you enter a civil union, your domestic partnership is automatically terminated. In addition, since 2/19/2007, new domestic partnerships are not allowed for people under 62.) Either form of partnership gives the surviving partner the right to inherit from the deceased partner and treats survivors like spouses for inheritance tax purposes.
New York	Does not offer same-sex marriage or domestic partnership benefits, but recognizes valid same-sex marriages performed elsewhere.
Oregon	Registered domestic partners are given most of the rights that married couples have, including inheritance rights.
Vermont	Same-sex couples are allowed to marry. The state also offers civil unions that give partners all the rights of married couples under state law, including inheritance rights. Although it is technically possible that you can be both married and in a civil union under Vermont law, to avoid confusion we ask you to choose one status or the other when you make your will. Doing so will not affect the way your property is distributed after your death.
Washington	Registered domestic partners are given many of the same rights as married couples, including inheritance rights. Washington's community property laws do not apply to domestic partners.

If you're married. When making your will, you may not be sure whether you should identify yourself as married or single, given that some states recognize your marriage and others don't. But either way, your document will be valid, and you can leave your property as you wish, subject to your spouse's rights.

If you and your partner live in a state that recognizes same-sex marriages, simply state that you are married. Your document will refer to your partner as your spouse.

If you got married and then moved to a state that doesn't recognize same-sex marriages, you can still state that you're married when you make your will. Even if your current state doesn't acknowledge your marriage, your partner will receive everything that your will directs. You may want to attach a signed letter to your will that expresses your wish that your partner be treated in all ways as your legal spouse. You can find a sample in Chapter 11.

> **SEE AN EXPERT**
>
> **If you're not sure of your marital status.** If you're confused about the legal status of your relationship, you're not alone. A good estate planning lawyer who specializes in issues affecting gay and lesbian couples can provide you with the latest information for your state and answer questions about making the best estate plan for your situation.

If you registered your partnership in the state where you live. If you and your partner registered as partners in a state that offers benefits to same-sex couples and you still live in that state, choose "I have a registered domestic partner," when asked for your relationship status. Although some states use different terms (such as "civil union partners" or "reciprocal beneficiaries") we generally use "domestic partners" to refer to a registered same-sex couple. If you live in a state that uses another term, your finished document will contain the correct term for your state. (If you live in New Jersey, where you may have a domestic partnership or a civil union, you will be asked to select the appropriate term for your relationship.)

If you have not registered your partnership in the state where you live.
If you and your partner have not registered with your state or if you
no longer live in the state where you registered, you should make your
will as a single person by choosing "I'm not married, nor do I have a
registered domestic partner."

Indicating that you are single does not limit your ability to leave
property to your partner or to name your partner as executor of your
will or guardian of your young children. You can do all of those things
in your will.

> RESOURCE
>
> **More information for same-sex couples.** For complete information
> about the legal issues that same-sex couples face, see *A Legal Guide for Lesbian &
> Gay Couples*, by Denis Clifford, Frederick Hertz and Emily Doskow (Nolo).

Your Spouse or Domestic Partner

Quicken WillMaker prompts you to provide the full name of your
spouse or domestic partner. As with your own name, list all names used
for business purposes, following the tips suggested for entering your own
name, above.

Also indicate whether your spouse or domestic partner is male or
female. This way, the program can refer to him or her with the correct
pronoun.

Your Children

Becoming a parent is what may have motivated you to buckle down to
the task of writing your will in the first place.

If you are the parent of young children, your will is the perfect place
to address some driving concerns you are likely to have if you die before
they are grown. These concerns include:

- who will care for your children, and
- who will manage their property.

Quicken WillMaker lets you make these decisions separately. This gives you the option of placing the responsibilities in the hands of the same person or, if need be, naming different people. First, you are asked to name someone to care for your children. Later in the program, you'll deal with the issue of providing property management for your own or other people's young children. (See Chapter 6.)

Identifying Your Children

Quicken WillMaker asks you whether or not you have any children and, if you do, it asks you to name each of them. You are not required to leave property to your children, but it is important that you at least state each child's name. If you don't, it may not be clear whether you intentionally left a child out of your will, or whether the child was accidentally overlooked (called "pretermitted," under the law). Children unintentionally omitted from your will—usually because you made your will before they were born—have a right to take a share of your estate.

> **SEE AN EXPERT**
> **Children born after a parent dies.** If a child is conceived before your death but is born after you die, he or she will most likely be entitled to part of your estate even if your will doesn't mention the child. But the law is now rushing to answer a new question posed by advancing medical technology: What happens if a child is conceived *after* the death of a parent? If sperm, eggs or embryos are preserved before the parent's death, a child could be born years later. Individual states are taking different approaches to this matter. Some are giving posthumously conceived children the rights to inherit property and receive other benefits from their deceased parents. Others are refusing such rights. If you are curious about this issue or planning for a posthumously conceived child, you should consult a knowledgeable estate planning lawyer.

When naming your children, you should include all children born to you or legally adopted by you.

If you are the parent of a child who has been legally adopted by a person other than your spouse or partner—or you have otherwise given up your legal parental rights—then you need not name that child in your will.

You should not name stepchildren you have not adopted, since they are not entitled by law to a share of your property when you die. The pretermitted heir rule does not apply to them. Also, Quicken WillMaker offers a number of options that include your children as a group, and if you include stepchildren in the list and use one of these options, your will might contain provisions you did not intend.

However, you are free to leave your stepchildren as much property in your will as you wish. If you want to treat your children and stepchildren equally and not differentiate between them, when Quicken WillMaker asks how you wish to leave your property, choose the option labeled "Leave it some other way." (See Chapter 5.)

To list your children, enter their full names in the sequence and format you want the names to appear in your will.

> **CAUTION**
>
> **Don't use "all my children."** Some people are tempted to skimp on naming their children individually and want to fill in "all my children," "my surviving children," "my lawful heirs" or "my issue." Don't do it. That shorthand language is much more confusing than listing each child by name.

Your Children's Birthdates

Quicken WillMaker also asks you to enter your children's dates of birth—month, day and year. The program will automatically compute their ages in years—an important consideration when you are asked to name a personal guardian and provide management for property you or others leave them.

Personal Guardians for Your Minor Children

Among the most pressing concerns of parents with minor children is who will care for the children if one or both of them die before the children reach adulthood.

Although contemplating the possibility of your early death can be wrenching, it is important to face up to it and adopt the best contingency plan for the care of your young children. If the other parent is available, then he or she can usually handle the task.

However, you and the other parent might die close together in time. Or you may currently be a single parent and need to decide what will happen if you do not survive until your children become adults.

This section discusses using Quicken WillMaker to choose a personal guardian to care for the children's basic health, education and other daily needs. Choosing a person to manage your children's property is discussed in Chapter 6.

Reasons for Naming a Personal Guardian

The general legal rule is that if there are two parents willing and able to care for the children and one dies, the other will take over physical custody and responsibility for caring for the child. In many states, the surviving parent may also be given authority by a court to manage any property the deceased parent left to the children—unless the deceased parent has specified a different property management arrangement in a will.

But there is no ready fallback plan if both parents of a minor child die or, in the case of a single parent, there is not another parent able or willing to do the job. Using Quicken WillMaker, you can deal with these concerns by naming a personal guardian as well as an alternate. The person you name will normally be appointed by the court to act as a surrogate parent for your minor children if both of the following are true:

- There is no surviving biological or adoptive parent able to properly care for the children.
- The court agrees that your choice is in the best interests of the children.

If both parents are making wills, each should name the same person as guardian for each child. This will help avoid the possibility of a dispute and perhaps even a court battle should the parents die simultaneously. But remember, if one parent dies, the other will usually assume custody and will then be free to make a new will naming a different personal guardian if he or she wishes. In short, if both parents are active caretakers, the personal guardian named in a will cares for the children only if both parents die close together in time.

However, if you feel strongly that the other parent is not the best person to care for the children, be sure to explain your reasoning when the Quicken WillMaker program prompts you to do so. (See "Explaining Your Choice," below.)

Naming Different Guardians for Different Children

One obvious concern when choosing a personal guardian for your children is to keep them together if they get along well with one another. This suggests that it is best to name the same personal guardian for all the children.

There are families, however, where the children are not particularly close to one another but have strong attachments with one or more adults outside the immediate family. For instance, one child may spend a lot of time with a grandparent while another child may be close to an aunt and uncle. Also, in a second or third marriage, a child from an earlier marriage may be closer to a different adult than a child from the current marriage.

In these situations and others, logic dictates other advice: Choose the personal guardian you believe would best be able to care for the child. This may mean that you will choose different personal guardians for different children.

Choosing a Personal Guardian

To qualify as a personal guardian, your choice must be an adult—18 in most states—and competent to do the job. For obvious reasons, you should first consider an adult with whom the child already has a close relationship—a stepparent, grandparent, aunt or uncle, older sibling, babysitter, close friend of the family or even neighbor. Whomever you choose, be sure that person is mature, good-hearted and willing and able to assume the responsibility.

Naming More Than One Person as Guardian

In many cases, it's a poor idea to name more than one person to serve as guardian for your children. Naming multiple guardians raises the possibility that they may disagree about the best way to raise a child, resulting in conflict and perhaps even requiring court intervention. However, there is one situation in which naming two guardians makes good sense: when you want to name a couple to care for your children together.

If you know a couple—for example, your sister and her husband— who are willing and able to take good care of your children, it's fine to name them both as coguardians. The couple will act as your children's surrogate parents. Both of them will be allowed to do things for your children that require legal authority, such as picking up your children from school, authorizing field trips or taking them to the doctor.

Keep in mind, however, that if you name a couple as coguardians, they must be able to agree on what's best for your children. Any severe difference of opinion between them could require court intervention— and this would be difficult for the couple and upsetting to your kids. Also, if you name a couple that parts ways while you are still alive, you should revise your will to name one or the other to care for your children or choose a different couple to act as coguardians.

The main point is that you must choose carefully when naming a couple as personal coguardians for your children. Select a couple that can make joint decisions without conflict, has a unified parenting style and is likely to stay together a long time. If you have any reservations about the longevity of the couple's relationship or any concerns about either person's parenting style, you may be better off just naming one of them—for example, name just your sister. If you like, you can explain the reasons for your choice in your will. See "Explaining Your Choice," below.

Choosing an Alternate Personal Guardian

Quicken WillMaker lets you name a backup or alternate personal guardian to serve in case your first choice for each child either changes his or her mind or is unable to do the job at your death. The considerations involved in naming an alternate personal guardian are the same as those you pondered when making your first choice: maturity, a good heart, familiarity with the children and willingness to serve.

If you name a couple as coguardians, the alternate will become the personal guardian only if both coguardians are unable or unwilling to serve.

Explaining Your Choice

Leaving a written explanation of why you made a particular choice for a personal guardian may be especially important if you think a judge may have reason to question your decision.

If you don't want the other parent to have custody. You may have strong ideas about why the child's other parent, or perhaps a grandparent, should not have custody of your minor children. In an age when many parents live separately, the following predicaments are sadly common:

- "I have custody of my three children. I don't want my ex-husband, who I believe is emotionally destructive, to get custody of our children if I die. Can I choose a guardian to serve instead of him?"
- "I have legal custody of my daughter and I've remarried. My present wife is a much better mother to my daughter than my ex-wife, who never cared for her properly. What can I do to make sure my present wife gets custody if I die?"
- "I live with a man who's been a good parent to my children for six years. My father doesn't like the fact that we aren't married and may well try to get custody of the kids if I die. What can I do to see that my partner gets custody?"

There is no definitive answer to these questions. If you die while the child is still a minor and the other parent disputes your choice in court, the judge will likely grant custody to the other parent, unless that parent:

- has legally abandoned the child by not providing for or visiting the child for an extended period, or
- is clearly unfit as a parent.

It is usually difficult to prove that a parent is unfit, absent serious and obvious problems such as chronic drug or alcohol abuse, mental illness or a history of child abuse. The fact that you do not like or respect the other parent is never enough, by itself, for a court to deny custody to him or her.

> **EXAMPLE:** Susan and Fred, an unmarried couple, have two minor children. Although Susan loves Fred, she does not think he is capable of raising the children on his own. She uses Quicken WillMaker to name her mother, Elinor, as guardian. If Susan dies, Fred, as the children's other parent, will be given first priority as personal guardian over Elinor, despite Susan's will, assuming the court finds he is willing and able to care for the children. However, if the court finds that Fred should not be personal guardian, Elinor would get the nod, assuming she is fit.

If you honestly believe the other natural parent is incapable of caring for your children properly—or simply will not assume the responsibility—you should reinforce that belief by explaining why you elected to name other people as guardians and alternates.

> **EXAMPLE:** Justine and Paul live together with Justine's minor children from an earlier marriage. The biological father is out of the picture, but Justine fears that her mother, Tamira, who does not approve of unmarried couples living together, will try to get custody of the kids if something happens to her. Justine wants Paul to have custody because he knows the children well and loves them. She can use Quicken WillMaker to name Paul as personal guardian and add a statement making the reasons for this choice clear.

If Justine dies and Tamira goes to court to get custody, the fact that Justine named Paul will give him an advantage. If he is a good parent, he is likely to get custody in most states.

Tips on What to Include

When deciding who should become a child's personal guardian, the courts of all states are required to act in the child's best interests. In making this determination, the courts commonly consider a number of facts, which you might want to include when explaining your choice for personal guardian. They include:

- whom the parents nominated to become the personal guardian
- whether the proposed personal guardian will provide the greatest stability and continuity of care for the child
- which person will best be able to meet the child's needs, whatever these happen to be
- the quality of the relationship between the child and the adults being considered for guardian
- the child's preferences to the extent these can be gleaned, and
- the moral fitness and conduct of the proposed guardians.

If you name your same-sex partner as guardian. If you coparent your children with a same-sex partner, you probably want to nominate your partner as the personal guardian of your children. Whether or not the court will respect your nomination depends on where you live and on two legal relationships: the relationship between you and your partner and the relationship between your partner and your kids.

If your children have another legal parent, perhaps from a prior relationship, the court will choose that parent over your partner unless you provide a good reason not to.

If you live in any of the states that recognize same-sex marriage or marriage-like relationships (such as registered domestic partnerships or civil unions) and your children were born after you and your partner entered into a legal relationship under the laws of that state, then you and your partner are both legal parents under state law and the court should respect your partner's legal right to continue parenting your children after your death. This is true whether or not you nominate your partner in your will, but you should go ahead and make the nomination and explain your reasons for it, as discussed below.

If you live in a state that doesn't offer any legal relationship for same-sex couples, the court will make the final decision about who will care for your children. The court will consider your choice for personal guardian, but it may not understand or fully respect your relationship with your partner.

For these reasons, take advantage of the opportunity to fully explain to the court why you named your partner to care for your children. You might say, for example, "I name my life partner, Ruth Williams, as the personal guardian for our son Matthew Price because we conceived and raised him together and she is his only other parent." Or, "I name my domestic partner, Richard Bennett, as personal guardian for our daughter Jane Bennett-Hines because he is her other legal parent, as recognized by the state of California."

RESOURCE

Learn more about same-sex families. For a detailed discussion of parenting issues for same-sex couples, see *A Legal Guide for Lesbian & Gay Couples*, by Denis Clifford, Frederick Hertz and Emily Doskow (Nolo).

Your Grandchildren

Quicken WillMaker asks you to name your grandchildren. Name all of them—including those to whom you leave no property. Include children adopted by your child and those born while your child was not married.

It is important that you name all grandchildren, because the rule that allows unintentionally omitted children to take a share of your estate also applies to grandchildren you may have overlooked in your will if their parent—that is, your child—dies before you do. (See "Your Children," above.)

As it does for your own children, Quicken WillMaker automatically provides the statement that if you have not left any property to a grandchild, that is intentional—and therefore eliminates the problem. Again, you are free to leave the grandchild property if you choose. Also, if you have additional grandchildren after making your will, it is wise to make a new will that includes them.

Keep Your Will Current

Here are two situations in which you should make a new will:

If a child is born to or legally adopted by you after you make your will. You should draft a new will to list the new child. If you do not, that child may challenge your will and receive a share of what you leave.

If one of your children dies before you do and leaves children of his or her own. The laws of many states require that you name and provide for the children of deceased children. If you do not, they may be considered accidentally overlooked and entitled to part of your property. To protect against this, make a new will, naming these grandchildren so that you can signal that you are aware that these grandchildren exist. You are still free to leave them as little or as much property as you wish in your will.

(See Chapter 10 for information on updating your will.)

SEE AN EXPERT

If you don't know your family. If family estrangement or other circumstances leave you thinking that you might not know the names of all of your grandchildren—or even your children—seek the advice of a good estate planning lawyer. You'll want to be certain that your will is not subject to unexpected claims.

Pets

You can use the Quicken WillMaker will to leave your pet to a caretaker you choose. You can also leave money to that person to help with the costs of caring for your pet, although your will cannot force the caretaker to use the money that way. If you want the caretaker to be legally bound to use the money for the care of your pet, you will need a pet trust. See "Setting up a trust for your pet," below.

Using a will to provide for your pet is a simple and inexpensive way to make sure your pet has a caring home after your death. It is not the only way to provide for your pet, but most folks find that it makes the most sense.

Leaving Details About Your Pet's Care

In addition to naming a caretaker for your pet, you may want to leave information and suggestions about your pet's habits and needs. You can use Quicken WillMaker's Information for Survivors and Caregivers form for this purpose. It allows you to leave specifics about each animal, including health needs, food and exercise requirements and sleeping habits. You can also use the document to describe memorial plans or final arrangements for your pet.

SEE AN EXPERT

Setting up a trust for your pet. In a majority of states, you can leave your pet money in a trust, managed by a trustee you name. You'll need to hire an attorney to be sure the document is properly drafted and valid in your state.

Finding a Loving Home for Your Pet

If you're not able to find someone both willing and able to take care of your pet after you die, you're not without options. More and more programs are springing up across the country to help assure people that their pets will have a loving home when they can no longer care for them.

SPCA programs. The San Francisco SPCA was the first to offer a special service to find good homes for the pets of its deceased members. The pets' new owners are entitled to free lifetime veterinary care for the pets at the SPCA's hospital. Other SPCAs have created similar programs. Contact local SPCAs and similar organizations in your area for more information.

Veterinary school programs. A number of veterinary schools take in pets whose owners leave substantial endowments to the school. These programs typically provide a homelike atmosphere and lifetime veterinary care for the animals. Here is a list of some schools that you can contact:

California
Center for Companion Animal Health
UC Davis School of Veterinary
    Medicine
530-752-7024
www.vetmed.ucdavis.edu/CCAH/TLC

Indiana
Peace of Mind Program
School of Veterinary Medicine, Purdue
    University
800-830-0104
www.vet.purdue.edu/giving/giving/
    peaceofmind.html

Kansas
Perpetual Pet Care Program
Kansas State University School of
    Veterinary Medicine
785-532-5560
www.vet.k-state.edu/depts/
    development/perpet/index

Minnesota
PerPETual Pet Care Program
University of Minnesota College of
    Veterinary Medicine
612-624-1247
www.cvm.umn.edu/devalumni/
    perpetualcare/home.html

Oklahoma
Cohn Family Shelter for Small Animals
Oklahoma State University, Center for
    Veterinary Health Sciences
405-744-6728
www.cvhs.okstate.edu

Texas
Stevenson Companion Animal Life-
    Care Center
College of Veterinary Medicine, Texas
    A&M University
979-845-1188
www.cvm.tamu.edu/petcare

About Your Property

T his chapter discusses the grist of will making: what you own, how you own it and what legal rules affect how you can leave it. Once you have considered the information about property in this chapter, you will be ready to use Quicken WillMaker to leave it to others—a task discussed in detail in Chapter 5. If you have children, see Chapter 6 for a discussion of their right to inherit property and your right to disinherit them.

Many readers will not need the information in this chapter. If you plan to leave your property in a lump—that is, without giving specific items of property to specific people—it makes little difference what you own and how you own it. That will be sorted out when you die, and the people you have named to take "all" your property will get whatever you own.

This chapter is important for you to read if either of the following is true:

- You are married or in a registered domestic partnership and you plan to name someone other than your spouse or partner to receive all or most of your property. This includes everyone who has not received a final decree of divorce or dissolution.
- You plan to leave specific items of property to specific people or organizations.

TIP

Keeping track of your property. There are many things your survivors will need to know about your property—and it will help them to have some relevant information about it, including:

- the location of some items
- the location of ownership, warranty and appraisal papers
- the value of some items—especially if they have special significance
- directions for maintaining the property, and
- details about caring for your pets.

You can use Quicken WillMaker's Information for Caregivers and Survivors form for this task.

Inventory Your Valuable Property

The first step is to take inventory—write down the valuable items of property you own. The categories listed below should jog your memory.

Even if you plan to leave everything to your spouse or children, you should make a list. It will help you to avoid overlooking things. And if you make a trust, every item (or group of items) must be specifically described and listed in the trust document.

To help you with this task, Quicken WillMaker provides a property worksheet that you can print out and keep with you as a reference while you make your estate planning documents. You can access the property worksheet from the screen called "Leaving Your Property," which introduces you to the topic of leaving your property to others. Click on the "Property Worksheet" link to start making your list.

Property You Should Not Include in Your Will

In almost all cases, your will does not affect property that you have arranged to leave by another method. (There's an exception in the state of Washington; see below.)

Property with a right of survivorship. If you hold property in joint tenancy, tenancy by the entirety or community property with right of survivorship, your share of that property automatically belongs to the surviving co-owner after you die. A will provision leaving your share would have no effect unless all co-owners die simultaneously.

Property you place in a trust. Property you place in a trust passes automatically to the beneficiary named in the trust document; you cannot pass this property in your will. This includes property placed in a revocable living trust. (To learn more about living trusts, see Chapter 12.)

Property for which you've already named a beneficiary. There are many ways to pass property without a will or trust. You shouldn't include in your will any type of property on this this list.

- Money in a pay-on-death bank account. If you want to change the beneficiary, contact the financial institution.

Valuable Property

Animals

Antiques

Appliances

Art

Books

Business interests
  Sole proprietorship
  Partnership
  Corporation
  LLC

Business property*

Cameras and photo
  equipment

Cash accounts
  Certificates of
    deposit
  Checking
  Money market
    funds
  Savings

China, crystal and
  silver

Coins and stamps

Collectibles

Computers

Copyrights, patents
  and trademarks

Electronic
  equipment

Furniture

Furs

Jewelry

Limited partnership

Precious metals

Real estate
  Agricultural land
  Boat/marina dock
    space
  Co-ops
  Condos
  Duplexes
  Houses
  Mobile homes
  Rental property
  Time-shares
  Undeveloped land
  Vacation houses

Retirement accounts

Royalties

Securities
  Bonds
  Commodities
  Mutual funds
  Stocks
  U.S. bills, notes and
    bonds

Tools

Vehicles
  Bicycles
  Cars
  Motorcycles
  Motor homes/RVs
  Planes
  Boats

---

* If you own a sole proprietorship

- Property held in beneficiary (transfer-on-death or TOD) form. This may include stocks, bonds and—in a handful of states—real estate or vehicles. To change the beneficiary, you'll need to make a new beneficiary form, deed or title document.
- Proceeds of a life insurance or annuity policy for which you've named a beneficiary. To make changes, contact the insurance company.
- Money in a pension plan, individual retirement account (IRA), 401(k) plan or other retirement plan. You name the beneficiary on forms provided by the account administrator.

To learn more about these property ownership methods, most of which are designed to avoid probate court proceedings, see Chapter 12.

Note for Washington Readers

The state of Washington has changed some of the rules discussed above. If you like, you can leave the following types of property in your will:

- your share of joint tenancy bank accounts
- pay-on-death bank accounts
- transfer-on-death securities or security accounts, and
- property in a living trust.

If you set up one of these devices for leaving your property and then later use your will to change the beneficiary, the property goes to the person you name in your will. However, if you designate a new beneficiary after you make your will—for example, by updating the paperwork for a pay-on-death account or changing your living trust—the gift in the will has no effect. (Wash. Rev. Code § 11.11.020.)

Property You Own With Others

If you are not married or in a registered domestic partnership, and you own property with someone else, you probably own it in tenancy in common. This is the most common way for unmarried people to own property together. Each co-owner is free to sell or give away his or her interest during life or leave it to another at death in a will. To tell whether or not you own property as tenancy in common, check the deed or other title document; it should specifically note that the property is held as a tenancy in common.

> **CAUTION**
> **More rules for married or legally partnered people making wills.**
> If you are married or in a registered domestic partnership, a whole host of legal rules may affect what property you own jointly and separately. (See "Property Ownership Rules for Married People," below.)

Property on Which You Owe Money

Using Quicken WillMaker, if you leave property on which you owe money, the beneficiary who takes it at your death will also take over the debt owed on that property. This means the beneficiary of the property is responsible for paying off the debt. (But your survivors will not inherit your debt, per se. For example, if you die with nothing to your name except credit card debt, your survivors will not be responsible for paying those bills.)

Property Ownership Rules for Married People

Most people who are married or are in registered domestic partnerships leave all or the greatest share of their property to their surviving spouses or partners. For them, the nuances of marital property law are not important, since the survivor gets the property anyway.

But if you plan to leave your property to several people instead of, or in addition to, your spouse or partner, the picture becomes more complicated. Under your state's laws, your spouse or partner may own some property you believe is yours. And if you do not own it, you cannot give it away—either now or at your death. Questions of which spouse or partner owns what property are important if your spouse or partner does not agree to your plan for property disposition.

There are two issues to consider:

- What do you own?
- Will your spouse or partner have the right to claim a share of your property after your death? (See "Your Spouse's Right to Inherit from You," below.)

This section will help you determine what you own and so can leave to others in your will. To figure it out, you need to know a little about the laws in your state. When it comes to property ownership, states are broadly divided into two types: community property states and common law property states.

Community Property States		
Alaska[1]	Louisiana	Texas
Arizona	Nevada	Washington
California[2]	New Mexico	Wisconsin
Idaho		

[1] If the couple makes a written agreement stating that they wish their property to be treated as community property.

[2] Registered domestic partners are also covered by community property laws.

Common Law States
All other states

Community Property States

If you live in a community property state, there are a few key rules to keep in mind while making your will:

- You can leave your separate property to anyone you wish.
- You can leave half of the community property (property you and your spouse or partner own together) to anyone you wish.
- After your death, your spouse or partner automatically keeps his or her half of the community property.
- If you are in a registered domestic partnership in California, all of the community property rules that apply to married couples also apply to you and your partner.

Another Option:
Community Property With Right of Survivorship

Alaska, Arizona, California, Nevada, Texas and Wisconsin allow a form of community property that works just like joint tenancy; in other words, the surviving spouse or domestic partner automatically inherits the property when the other spouse or partner dies. To take advantage of this type of ownership, the property's title document must state that the property is owned "as community property with right of survivorship," or something similar.

Your Separate Property

The following property qualifies as separate property in all community property states:

- property that you own before marriage
- property that you receive after marriage by gift or inheritance
- property that you purchase entirely with your separate property, and
- property that you earn or accumulate after permanent separation.

In some states, additional types of property—such as personal injury awards received by one spouse during marriage—may also qualify as separate property. (See "Property That Is Difficult to Categorize," below.)

Community property states differ in how they treat income earned from separate property. Most hold that such income is separate. But a number of states take the opposite approach, treating income from separate property as community property.

Normally, separate property stays separate as long as it is not:

- so mixed with marital property that it is impossible to tell what is separate and what is not, or
- transferred in writing by the separate property owner into a form of shared ownership.

Just as separate property can be transformed into shared property, community property can be turned into separate property by a gift from one spouse to the other. The rules differ somewhat from state to state, but, generally speaking, gifts made to transform one type of property into another must be made with a signed document.

Community Property

The basic rule of community property is simple: During a marriage, all property earned or acquired by either spouse or domestic partner is owned 50-50 by each spouse or partner, except for property received by only one of them through gift or inheritance.

More specifically, community property usually includes:

- All income received by either spouse or partner from employment or any other source (except gifts to or inheritance by just one spouse or partner)—for example, wages, stock options, pensions and other employment compensation and business profits. This rule generally applies only to the period when the couple lives together as husband and wife or domestic partners. Most community property states consider income and property acquired after the spouses or partners permanently separate to be the separate property of the spouse or partner who receives it.
- All property acquired with community property income during the marriage.

Classifying Property in Community Property States: Some Examples		
Property	**Community or Separate**	**Why**
A painting you inherited while married	Separate; you can leave it in your will.	Inherited property belongs only to the person who inherited it.
A car you bought before you got married	Separate; you can leave it in your will.	Property owned before marriage is not community property.
A boat you bought with your income while married and registered in your name	Community; you can leave only your half-interest in your will.	It was purchased with community property income (income earned during the marriage).
The family home you and your spouse own together	Community; you can leave only your half-interest in your will.	It was purchased with community property income (income earned during the marriage).
A loan that your brother owes you	Community; you can leave only your half-interest in your will.	The loan was made from community property funds and belongs half to you and half to your spouse.
A fishing cabin you inherited from your father	Separate; you can leave it in your will.	Inherited property belongs only to the person who inherited it.
Stock you and your spouse bought with savings from your spouse's earnings	Community; you can leave only your half-interest in your will.	It was purchased with one spouse's earnings, which are community property during marriage.

- All separate property that is transformed into community property under state law. This transformation can occur in several ways, including when one spouse or domestic partner makes a gift of separate property to both of them or when property is so mixed together that it's no longer possible to tell what property is separate (lawyers call this "commingling").
- As mentioned above, in a few community property states, income earned during marriage from separate property—for example, rent, interest or dividends—is community property. Most community property states consider such income to be separate property, however.

EXAMPLE: Beth and Daniel live in Idaho, one of the few community property states where income earned from separate property belongs to the community. Beth inherits 22 head of Angus cattle from her father. Those cattle go on to breed a herd of more than 100 cattle. All the descendants of the original 22 animals are considered income from Beth's separate property and are included in the couple's community property estate.

Property That Is Difficult to Categorize

Normally, classifying property as community or separate property is easy. But in some situations, it can be a close call. There are several potential problem areas.

Businesses. Family businesses can create complications, especially if they were owned before marriage by one spouse or domestic partner and expanded during the marriage or partnership. The key is to figure out whether the increased value of the business is community or separate property. If you and your spouse or partner do not have the same view of how to pass on the business, it may be worthwhile to get help from a lawyer or accountant.

Money from a personal injury lawsuit. Usually, but not always, awards won in a personal injury lawsuit are the separate property of the spouse or partner receiving them. There is no easy way to characterize this type of property. If a significant amount of your property came from a personal injury settlement, research the specifics of your state's law or ask an estate planning expert.

Pensions. Generally, for married people, the part of a pension gained from earnings made during the marriage is considered to be community property. This is also true of military pensions. However, some federal pensions—such as Railroad Retirement benefits and Social Security retirement benefits—are not considered community property, because federal law deems them to be the separate property of the employee earning them. Also, because the federal government does not recognize domestic partnerships, community property rules will not apply to federal benefits acquired by registered domestic partners.

Common Law Property States

Common law property states are all states other than the community property states listed above.

In these states, you own:

- all property you purchased using your property or income, and
- property you own solely in your name if it has a title slip, deed or other legal ownership document.

In common law states, the key to ownership for many types of valuable property is whose name is on the title. If you and your spouse or registered domestic partner take title to a house together—that is, both of your names are on the deed—you both own it. That is true even if you earned or inherited the money you used to buy it. If your spouse or domestic partner earns the money, but you take title in your name alone, you own it.

If the property is valuable but has no title document, such as a computer, then the person whose income or property is used to pay for it owns it. If joint income is used, then you own it together. You can each leave your half in your will, unless you signed an agreement providing for a joint tenancy or a tenancy by the entirety.

EXAMPLE: Will and Jane are married and live in Kentucky, a common law property state. They have five children. Shortly after their marriage, Jane wrote an extremely popular computer program that helps doctors diagnose illness. She has received royalties averaging about $200,000 a year over a ten-year period. Jane has used the royalties to buy a car, boat and mountain cabin—all registered in her name alone. The couple also owns a house as joint tenants. In addition, Jane owns a number of family heirlooms which she inherited from her parents. Throughout their marriage, Jane and Will have maintained separate savings accounts. Will works as a computer engineer and has deposited all of his income into his account. Jane put her unspent royalties in her account, which now contains $75,000.

Jane owns:
- the savings account listed in her name alone
- one-half interest in the house (which, because it is held in joint tenancy, will go to Will at Jane's death)
- the car, boat and cabin, since there are title documents listing them in her name (if there were no such documents, she would still own them because they were bought with her income), and
- her family heirlooms.

Will owns:
- the savings account listed in his name alone, and
- one-half interest in the house (which, because it is held in joint tenancy, will go to Jane at Will's death).

EXAMPLE: Martha and Scott, who are married, have both worked for 30 years as schoolteachers in Michigan, a common law state. Generally, Scott and Martha pooled their income and jointly purchased a house, worth $200,000 (in both their names as joint tenants); cars (one in Martha's name and one in Scott's); a share in a vacation condominium (in both names as joint tenants); and household furniture. Each maintains a separate savings account, and they also have a joint tenancy checking account containing $2,000. In addition, Scott and his sister own a piece of land as tenants in common.

Martha owns:
- her savings account
- half-interest in the house, the joint checking account and the condo (which, because they are held in joint tenancy, will go to Scott at her death)
- her car, and
- half the furniture.

Scott owns:
- his savings account
- half-interest in the house, the joint checking account and the condo (which, because they are held in joint tenancy, will go to Martha at his death)
- his car
- half the furniture, and
- a half-interest in the land he owns with his sister.

Moving From State to State

Complications may set in when a husband and wife acquire property in a common law property state and then move to a community property state. California, Idaho, Washington and Wisconsin treat the earlier-acquired property as if it had been acquired in the community property state. The legal term for this type of property is "quasi-community property." Wisconsin calls it "deferred marital property."

The other community property states do not recognize the quasi-community property concept for will-making purposes. Instead, they go by the rules of the state where the property was acquired. If you and your spouse move from a non-community property state into one of the states that recognizes quasi-community property, all of your property is treated according to community property rules. However, if you move to any of the other community property states from a common law state, you must assess your property according to the rules of the state where the property was acquired.

Couples who move from a community property state to a common law state face the opposite problem. Generally, each spouse retains one-half interest in the community property the couple accumulated while living in the community property state. However, if there is a conflict after your death, it can get messy; courts dealing with the issue have not been consistent.

SEE AN EXPERT

If you move. If you move from a community property state to a common law one, and you and your spouse have any disagreement as to who owns what, it may be wise to check with a lawyer. (See Chapter 13.)

SEE AN EXPERT

Same-sex couples. If you are moving from the state in which you registered your domestic partnership, there is a good chance that the state you are moving to will not recognize the property rights you received through your partnership status. You may want to consult a knowledgeable attorney in your new state to be sure you both fully understand your property rights and have an appropriate plan in place.

Your Spouse's Right to Inherit From You

If you intend to leave your spouse or registered domestic partner very little or no property, you may run into some legal roadblocks. All common law property states (see above) protect a surviving spouse or partner from being completely disinherited—and most assure that a spouse has the right to receive a substantial share of a deceased spouse's property. Community property states offer a different kind of protection.

Spousal Protection in Common Law States

In a common law state, a shortchanged surviving spouse or domestic partner usually has the option of either taking what the will provides, called "taking under the will," or rejecting the gift and instead taking the minimum share allowed by state law, called "taking against the will." In some states, your spouse or partner may have the right to inherit the family residence, or at least use it for his or her life. The Florida constitution, for example, gives a surviving spouse the deceased spouse's residence.

Laws protecting spouses and domestic partners vary among the states. In many common law property states, a spouse is entitled to one-third of the property left in the will. In a few, it is one-half. The exact amount of the spouse's minimum share may also depend on whether there are also minor children and whether the spouse has been provided for outside the will by trusts or other means.

> EXAMPLE: Leonard's will leaves $50,000 to his second wife, June, and the rest of his property, totaling $400,000, to May and April, his daughters from his first marriage. June can choose instead to receive her statutory share of Leonard's estate, which will be far more than $50,000. To the probable dismay of May and April, their shares will be substantially reduced; they will share what is left of Leonard's property after June gets her statutory share.

Of course, these are just options; a spouse who is not unhappy with the share he or she receives by will is free to let it stand. And in almost all states, one spouse or partner can give up all rights to inherit any property by completing and signing a waiver. If you want to make that type of arrangement, consult a lawyer. (See Chapter 13.)

SEE AN EXPERT

Leaving little to a spouse. If you do not plan to leave at least half of your property to your spouse or domestic partner in your will and have not provided for him or her generously outside your will, consult a lawyer.

Family Allowances

Some states provide additional, relatively minor protections for immediate family members. These vary from state to state in too much detail to discuss here. Generally, however, these devices attempt to ensure that your spouse and children are not left out in the cold after your death, by allowing them temporary protection (such as the right to remain in the family home for a short period) or funds (typically, living expenses while an estate is being probated).

In many common law states, how much the surviving spouse is entitled to receive depends on what that spouse receives both under the will and outside of the will—for example, through joint tenancy or a living trust—as well as what the surviving spouse owns. The total of all of these is called the augmented estate.

While the augmented estate concept is rather complicated, its purpose is easy to grasp. Basically, almost all property of both spouses is taken into account, and the surviving spouse gets a piece of the whole pie.

Spousal Protection in Community Property States

Most community property states do not give surviving spouses or registered domestic partners the right to take a share of the deceased spouse's or partner's estate. Instead, they try to protect spouses and domestic partners while both are still alive, by granting each spouse or partner half ownership of property and earnings either spouse or partner acquires during the marriage. (See "Community Property States," above.)

However, in a few states—under very limited circumstances—a surviving spouse or domestic partner may elect to take a portion of the deceased spouse's community or separate property. These laws are designed to prevent spouses and domestic partners from being either accidentally overlooked—for example, if one spouse or partner makes a will before marriage or partnership and forgets to change it afterward to include the new spouse or partner—or deliberately deprived of their fair share of property. These protections are available in Alaska (Alaska Stat. §§ 13.12.201 and following), California (California Prob. Code §§ 21610 and following), Idaho (Idaho Code §§ 15-2-202 and following), Washington (Wash. Rev. Code §§ 26.16.240 and following) and Wisconsin (Wis. Stat. §§ 861.02 and following). If you want to learn more about them, consult a lawyer. (See Chapter 13.)

How to Leave Your Property

The heart of will making is deciding who gets your property when you die. For many, this is an easy task: You want it all to go to your spouse or partner, your kids or your favorite charity. For others, it's a little more complicated—for example, you want most of your property to go to your spouse, partner, child or charity, but you also want certain items to go to other people. You may even have a fairly complicated scheme in mind that involves dividing your property among a number of people and organizations.

Chapter 4 introduced some basic concepts about your property and whether you can leave it to others in your will. This chapter explains how to put your plan into effect using the Quicken WillMaker program. If you want to leave all or most of your property to a loved one or favorite charity, the program offers you some shortcuts. Quicken WillMaker also accommodates more complex wishes.

After you name those who will get your property, Quicken WillMaker lets you name alternates—that is, who should get property if your first choices do not survive you.

You do not need to read all of this chapter to figure out how to write the will you want. Start with the discussion that is tailored to your situation:

- married or in a registered domestic partnership, with children
- married or in a registered domestic partnership, with no children
- not married or in a registered domestic partnership, and you have children, or
- not married or in a registered domestic partnership, and you have no children.

If You Are Married or in a Registered Domestic Partnership and You Have Children

Many married or partnered people have simple will-making needs. They want to leave all or most of their property to their spouses or partners. As alternates, they may want to choose their children, or name another person or organization. Quicken WillMaker lets you choose any of those paths easily. And if you do not want to make your spouse or partner the main beneficiary of your will, that option is available, too.

Choosing Beneficiaries

Quicken WillMaker prompts you to choose one of three approaches to leaving your property. You can:
- leave everything to your spouse or domestic partner
- leave most of your property, with some specific exceptions, to your spouse or domestic partner, or
- make a plan that may or may not include your spouse or domestic partner.

The third option offers flexibility. You should choose it if you want to divide up your property more evenly among a number of beneficiaries or if you want to give all or most of your property to someone other than your spouse or domestic partner. But if you do choose this approach to making your will, be sure that you understand the rules governing what you own and the rights of your spouse or partner. (See "Property Ownership Rules for Married People" and "Your Spouse's Right to Inherit From You" in Chapter 4.)

> **EXAMPLE:** Anne and Robert are a married couple with one young child. Anne wants a simple will, in which she leaves all of her property to Robert. She chooses the first option—everything to your spouse—to get a will that reflects her wishes.

> **EXAMPLE:** Arnie wants his wife to receive most of his property when he dies, but he has a valuable violin that he wants to go to his best friend, Eddie, and a coin collection that he wants his nephew to receive. Arnie chooses the second option—most to your spouse. Then, later in the program, he can name Eddie to receive his violin and his nephew to receive his coin collection.

> **EXAMPLE:** Sylvia is married to Fred. She wants to leave him her share of their investment portfolio and family business but also

wants to leave a number of specific property items to different friends, relatives and charities. She chooses the third option when using Quicken WillMaker. The program then prompts her to list specific property items and the person or organization she wants to receive each one. Before she does, Sylvia reviews Chapter 6 to make sure she understands what property is appropriate to leave in her will.

SKIP AHEAD

When you can skip ahead. If you do not want to name your spouse or registered domestic partner to receive all or most of your property, skip the rest of this section and go to "Making Specific Bequests," below, for a discussion of what comes next.

Choosing Alternates for Your Spouse or Partner

If you want your spouse or registered domestic partner to receive all or most of your property, your next task will be to choose an alternate for your spouse or partner.

The will you create with Quicken WillMaker provides that all beneficiaries—including your spouse—must survive you by 45 days to receive the property you leave them. This is a standard will provision, called a survivorship requirement. It is based on the assumption that if a beneficiary survives you by only a few days or weeks, you would prefer the property to go to another beneficiary that you choose and name in your will.

The alternates you choose will receive the property only if your spouse or domestic partner dies fewer than 45 days after you do.

Depending on your previous choices, Quicken WillMaker offers two or three options for alternates. You can name:

- your child or children, or
- other alternate beneficiaries.

These two approaches to naming alternates are shortcuts. You need not specify which items go to which beneficiaries.

If you named your spouse or domestic partner to receive all your property, you also have a third option: You can make a completely new plan for leaving your property which will take effect only if your spouse does not survive you by at least 45 days. If you make this choice, you can divide your property among a number of alternate beneficiaries.

Each of these approaches to naming alternates is discussed below.

Naming Your Children as Alternates

It is common for married or partnered people who have children to simply leave all or most of their property to the surviving spouse or partner and name the children to take the property as alternates. This means if your spouse or partner does not survive you by 45 days, the property your spouse or partner would have received will pass to your child or children.

If you have more than one child, you must decide how the children should share the property.

> **EXAMPLE:** Meg and Charlie have three grown children. When Charlie makes his will, he leaves everything to Meg and names the children as alternates for her. He directs that all three children should receive equal shares of his property if Meg doesn't survive him and they take it, instead.

If any of your children are minors or young adults, you may:

- specify the share each child will receive; later, you may designate how each child's share will be managed and doled out if a child is under 35 when you die, or
- direct that the property be held in one undivided fund, called a pot trust; under this option, the person you select to serve as trustee will use the assets in the trust for all your children as needed, until your youngest child turns an age you choose—up to age 25.

(See Chapter 6 for a discussion of these methods for managing property left to children.)

EXAMPLE: Julia and Emanuel have three young children. When Julia makes her will, she names Emanuel to inherit most of her property and leaves a few small items to her sister. As alternates for her husband, she picks her children. But because they are too young to manage money or property, later in the program she names her sister to manage any property the children may take under her will while they are still young.

EXAMPLE: Barry and his wife, Marta, have two young daughters close in age. In his will, Barry leaves Marta all his property and chooses the children as alternate beneficiaries. He also picks the pot trust option and names his mother as trustee. If Marta does not survive him by at least 45 days, all of Barry's property will go into a trust for the two girls, administered by Barry's mother.

Quicken WillMaker also lets you name a second level of alternates— that is, alternates who will take the property a child would have received, if that child does not survive you. You can name an alternate for each child or simply designate that the survivors receive any property that would have gone to a deceased child.

Naming Alternates Who Are Not Your Children

If you decide to specify alternates to receive the property left to your spouse or domestic partner, you may name whomever you want. You are not constrained, as with the first option, to naming only your children as alternates. For instance, you may name a charity, a friend or just one of your children. If your spouse or partner does not survive you by 45 days, the alternates you name will receive the property your spouse or partner would have received. If you name more than one person or organization, you may specify what share each is to receive.

EXAMPLE: Celeste is married with two grown children. The children have both been provided for nicely with money from trusts and are financially secure. In her will, Celeste leaves her husband most of her property, with a few exceptions of some heirlooms for her children. As an alternate for her husband, she names the university where she taught for many years.

You can also name a second level of alternates—that is, alternates to take the property should both your spouse or partner and a first level of alternates you name all die before you do. You can name a backup alternate for each alternate. If you named more than one first-level alternate, you may also designate that the survivors receive any property that would have gone to a deceased alternate.

Making a Different Plan

This option—Plan B—is available only if you choose to leave all your property to your spouse or registered domestic partner.

It lets you create a whole new plan to take effect if, and only if, your spouse or partner doesn't survive you by 45 days. This option is for people who think like this: I want to leave all my property to my spouse, period. But in case my spouse does not survive me, I want to make a whole new plan from the ground up—my Plan B—that does not include my spouse. So, if my spouse survives me, he or she gets all my property. But if not, I'll have been able to divide my property just as if I weren't married.

Your Plan B can include as many specific bequests as you wish. (See "Making Specific Bequests," below.) After you have made all your specific bequests, you can also name someone to take the rest of your property. This is called your residuary beneficiary. (See "Naming Residuary Beneficiaries," below.) Again, all of these Plan B bequests will take effect only if your spouse or domestic partner does not survive you by 45 days.

> EXAMPLE: Sean wants to leave all his property to Eva, his wife, if she's alive when he dies. But thinking about what he would want to happen if Eva were not around to take everything, he decides that he would want to divide his property among several friends, relatives and charities.
>
> When he sits down with Quicken WillMaker to make his will, Sean names Eva to get all his property. Then, when it's time to

name alternates, he chooses the Plan B option and leaves $10,000 to a local food bank, his piano to his niece and the rest of his property to his brother.

If You Do Not Name Alternates

If you leave your entire estate to one person or a group of people, you do not name alternate beneficiaries, and your primary beneficiaries do not survive you, then your estate will be distributed according to the laws of your state. (See "Dying Without a Will" in Chapter 1.)

If You Are Married or in a Registered Domestic Partnership and You Do Not Have Children

Many married or partnered people have simple will-making needs. They want to leave all or most of their property to their spouses or domestic partners. Then, as alternates, they may name one or more other people or organizations. Quicken WillMaker lets you choose this path easily. And if you do not want to make your spouse or partner the main beneficiary of your will, that option is available, too.

Choosing Beneficiaries

Quicken WillMaker prompts you to choose one of three approaches to leaving your property. You can:
- leave everything to your spouse or domestic partner
- leave most of your property, with some specific exceptions, to your spouse or domestic partner
- make a plan that may or may not include your spouse or domestic partner.

The third option offers flexibility. You should choose it if you want to divide up your property more evenly among a number of beneficiaries or if you want to give all or most of your property to someone other than your spouse or partner. If you choose it, be sure that you understand the rules governing what you own and the rights of your spouse or registered domestic partner. (See "Property Ownership Rule for Married People" and "Your Spouse's Right to Inherit From You" in Chapter 4.)

> **EXAMPLE:** Mark and Abby are a young married couple with no children. Mark wants simply to leave everything to Abby in his will. He chooses the first option—everything to your spouse—so that his will reflects his intentions.

> **EXAMPLE:** Paul wants his wife to receive most of his property when he dies, but he wants his golf clubs to go to his best friend, Eric, and wants his niece to take his photography equipment. Paul chooses the second option—most to your spouse. Then, later in the program, he can name Eric to receive his golf clubs and his niece to receive the photography equipment.

> **EXAMPLE:** Eleanor is married to William. She wants to leave William her share of their investment portfolio and family business, but also wants to leave a number of specific items to different friends, relatives and charities. She chooses the third option when using Quicken WillMaker—make a different plan. The program then prompts her to list specific property items and the person or organization she wants to receive each of them. Before she does, Eleanor reviews Chapter 4 to make sure she understands what property is appropriate to leave in her will.

SKIP AHEAD

When you can skip ahead. If you do not want to name your spouse or domestic partner to receive all or most of your property, skip the rest of this section and go to "Making Specific Bequests," below, for a discussion of what comes next.

Choosing Alternates for Your Spouse or Partner

If you want your spouse or domestic partner to receive all or most of your property, your next task will be to choose an alternate for your spouse or partner.

The will you create with Quicken WillMaker provides that all beneficiaries—including your spouse or domestic partner—must survive you by 45 days to receive the property you leave them. This is a standard will provision, called a survivorship requirement. It is based on the assumption that if a beneficiary survives you by only a few days or weeks, you would prefer the property to go to another beneficiary that you name in your will.

The alternates you choose will receive the property only if your spouse or partner does not live at least 45 days longer than you do.

The simplest ways to provide for an alternate are to name:

- one person or organization to receive everything your spouse or partner would have received, or
- more than one person or organization to share the property. If you go that route, the alternates will receive all the property that would have gone to your spouse or partner. You need not specify which items go to which beneficiaries.

Or you can make a new plan for leaving your property—Plan B—which will take effect only if your spouse or partner does not survive you by 45 days. If you choose to make a new plan, you can divide your property among several alternate beneficiaries.

These approaches to naming alternates are discussed below.

Naming Alternates for Your Spouse or Partner

You may name whomever you want as the alternate for your spouse or domestic partner. For instance, you may name a charity, friend or relative. If your spouse or partner does not survive you by 45 days, the alternates you name will receive the property your spouse or partner would have received. If you name more than one person or organization, you may specify what share each is to receive.

EXAMPLE: In her will, Sharon leaves most of her property to her husband, Alex, with a few exceptions of some small items for friends. As an alternate for Alex, she names the charity at which she volunteered for many years.

You can also name a second level of alternates—that is, alternates to take the property should both your spouse and alternate not survive you. You can name a backup alternate for each alternate. If you named more than one first-level alternate, you may designate that the survivors receive any property that would have gone to a deceased alternate.

Making a Different Plan

If you choose to leave all your property to your spouse or domestic partner, you can create a whole new plan to take effect if, and only if, your spouse or partner doesn't survive you by 45 days. This option is for people who think like this: I want to leave all my property to my spouse, period. But in case my spouse does not survive me, I want to make a whole new plan from the ground up—my Plan B—that does not include my spouse. So, if my spouse survives me, he or she gets all my property. But if not, I'll divide my property just as if I weren't married.

Your alternate plan—Plan B—can include as many specific bequests as you wish. (See "Making Specific Bequests," below.) After you have made all your specific bequests, you can also name someone to take the rest of your property. This is called your residuary beneficiary. (See "Naming Residuary Beneficiaries," below.) Again, all of these Plan B bequests will take effect only if your spouse or domestic partner does not survive you by 45 days.

EXAMPLE: Sean wants to leave all his property to Eva, his wife, if she's alive when he dies. But thinking about what he would want to happen if Eva were not around to take everything, he decides that he would want to divide his property among several friends, relatives and charities.

When he sits down with Quicken WillMaker to make his will, Sean names Eva to take everything. Then, when it's time to name alternates, he chooses the Plan B option and leaves $10,000 to a local food bank, his piano to his niece and everything else to his brother.

If You Do Not Name Alternates

If you leave your entire estate to one person or a group of people, you do not name alternate beneficiaries and your primary beneficiaries do not survive you, then your estate will be distributed according to the laws of your state. (See "Dying Without a Will" in Chapter 1.)

If You Are Not Married or in a Domestic Partnership and You Have Children

If you are a single parent, your children probably figure prominently in your plans for distributing your property after your death. With that in mind, Quicken WillMaker offers some shortcuts when making your will.

Choosing Beneficiaries

Quicken WillMaker prompts you to choose one of three approaches to leaving your property. You can:

- leave everything to your child or children
- leave most of your property, with some specific exceptions, to your child or children, or
- make a plan that may or may not include your children.

The third option offers flexibility. You should choose it if you want to divide your property more evenly among a number of beneficiaries, or if you want to give all or most of your property to someone other than your children. If you choose it, be sure that you understand the rules governing what you own. (See Chapter 4.)

> EXAMPLE: Raquel is a divorced mother of two young children. She wants to leave all her property to the children, in equal shares. She chooses the first option.

EXAMPLE: Carlo, a widower, has one son, who is now 40 years old. Carlo wants to leave most of his property to his son but also make a few small bequests to charities. He chooses the second option. Then, later in the program, he can name the charities and the amounts he wants to leave to each.

EXAMPLE: Brenda has three children, all of whom are grown and financially healthy. She wants to leave a number of specific property items to her children but also to many different friends, relatives and charities. She chooses the third option when using Quicken WillMaker. The program then asks her to list specific property items and the person or organization she wants to receive each one. Before doing this, Brenda reviews Chapter 4 to make sure she understands what property she can leave in her will.

SKIP AHEAD

When you can skip ahead. If you do not want to name your child or children to receive all or most of your property, skip the rest of this section and go to "Making Specific Bequests," below, for a discussion of what comes next.

Designating Children's Shares

If you have a number of children, you must decide how you want them to share the property they receive through your will.

EXAMPLE: Charlie has three grown children. When Charlie makes his will, he names the children to receive everything. He directs that all three children should receive equal shares of his property.

If any of your children are minors or young adults, you may:
• specify the share each child will receive; later, you may designate how each child's share will be managed and doled out if a child is under 35 when you die, or

- direct that the property be held in one undivided fund, called a pot trust; under this option, the person you select to serve as trustee will use the assets in the trust for all your children as needed, until your youngest child turns an age you choose up to age 25.

(See Chapter 6 for an explanation of all of these methods for managing property left to children.)

> **EXAMPLE:** Tess has three children, two teenagers and one 26-year-old son. When she makes her will, she leaves the children most of her property and leaves a few small items to her sister. Because her oldest child is self-supporting, she leaves him just a 1/5 share and leaves the two younger children 2/5 each. Later in the program, Tess names her sister to manage any property the two younger children come to own while they are still young.

> **EXAMPLE:** Frank has two young sons close in age. In his will, he leaves them all his property. He then picks the pot trust option and names his sister as trustee. That means that if the boys inherit Frank's property while they are still young, all of it will go into a trust for them, administered by Frank's sister.

Choosing Alternates for Your Children

If you choose your child or children to receive all or most of your property, your next task will be to choose an alternate for your child.

The will you create with Quicken WillMaker provides that a beneficiary must survive you by 45 days to receive property through the will. This is a standard will provision, called a survivorship requirement. It is based on the assumption that if a beneficiary survives you by only a few weeks, you would prefer the property to go to another beneficiary that you name in your will.

The alternates you choose for a child will receive the property only if the child does not survive you by at least 45 days.

> **CAUTION**
>
> **No alternates necessary for pot trusts.** If you chose a pot trust, you don't need to name alternates. If one child does not survive you, the other surviving children will still share the property.

If you have one child, you can either:

- name one or more alternates for that child, or
- make a plan that may or may not include your child and other people or organizations.

If you have more than one child and have designated a share for each child, you can either:

- name one or more alternates for each child, or
- specify that if one child doesn't survive you, the survivors should take the deceased child's share.

If you chose a pot trust, you need not name alternates. If any child does not survive you, the others will share the property.

Naming Alternates for Your Children

You may name whomever you want—for instance, a charity, friend or relative—as the alternate for a child. If the child does not survive you by 45 days, the alternates will receive the property the child would have received. If you name more than one alternate, you may specify the share each is to receive.

> **EXAMPLE:** In her will, Sharon leaves her daughter most of her property and gives the rest to friends. As an alternate for her daughter, she names her daughter's two young children.

Surviving Children

Rather than name alternates for each of your children, you may want to provide that whatever property you leave them will go to all the children who survive you.

EXAMPLE: In his will, Patrick leaves his daughter and two sons all of his property. He specifies that each should receive an equal share. When Quicken WillMaker asks him to name alternates for the children, he specifies that the survivors should take the share.

If You Do Not Name Alternates

If you leave your entire estate to one person or a group of people, you do not name alternate beneficiaries, and your primary beneficiaries do not survive you, then your estate will be distributed according to the laws of your state. (See "Dying Without a Will" in Chapter 1.)

If You Are Not Married or in a Domestic Partnership and You Do Not Have Children

As a single person, you are free to leave your property in any way you choose. Your beneficiaries may be your loved ones or organizations you value highly. You can divide your property as you see fit, whether that means leaving it all to one beneficiary or giving specific items to specific people. Or, you may prefer to combine these approaches, leaving most of your assets to one or more beneficiaries and a few unique items to others. In any case, you'll have the opportunity to choose alternate beneficiaries as well.

Choosing Beneficiaries

Quicken WillMaker prompts you to choose one of three approaches to leaving your property. You can:

- Leave everything to one or more beneficiaries. For example, you might leave everything you own to your girlfriend or to your sisters.
- Leave almost everything to one or more beneficiaries, but also leave some specific items to particular people. For example, you might want to leave all of your property to your sisters, but you want to leave your antique dining table to your neighbor.

- Leave your property some other way. You can leave specific items of property to certain beneficiaries, then choose one or more beneficiaries who will receive everything that's left. For example, you could leave your antique furniture to your sister, your ABC stock to your nephew, your comic book collection to your neighbor and everything else to the American Cancer Society.

If you want to leave specific items of property, be sure that you understand what kinds of property should be left in a will, and what might be passed to your survivors in other ways. (See "Property You Should Not Include in Your Will" in Chapter 4.)

> EXAMPLE: Fernando and Robert have been together for many years, but they do not live in a state that offers registered domestic partnerships. When Fernando makes his will, he wants all his property to go to Robert. He chooses the first option—leave everything to one person—to make a will that reflects his wishes.

> EXAMPLE: Theresa, whose husband died several years ago, wants to divide her money and possessions among different friends, relatives and charities. She chooses the third option. Quicken WillMaker then asks her to list specific property items and the person or organization she wants to receive each one. Then she names one person who will receive any other property that she owns at her death.

SKIP AHEAD

When you can skip ahead. If you do not want to name one or more beneficiaries to receive all or most of your property, skip the rest of this section and go to "Making Specific Bequests," below, for a discussion of what comes next.

Choosing Alternates

If you specify that one or more beneficiaries should receive all or most of your property, your next task will be to choose alternates.

The will you create with Quicken WillMaker provides that all beneficiaries must survive you by 45 days to receive the property you leave them. This is a standard will provision, called a survivorship requirement. It is based on the assumption that if a beneficiary survives you by only a few days or weeks, you would prefer the property to go to another beneficiary that you name in your will.

The alternates you choose will receive the property only if your main beneficiaries do not survive for at least 45 days after you die.

Quicken WillMaker offers two options for alternates. You can:

- name alternate beneficiaries, or
- make a completely new plan which will take effect only if your main beneficiaries do not survive you by 45 days. This way, you can divide your property among several alternate beneficiaries.

Naming Alternates

You may name whomever you want as alternates for each of your main beneficiaries. For instance, for each of your main beneficiaries, you may name a charity or a group of friends. If you name more than one person or organization, you may specify the share each is to receive.

If a main beneficiary does not survive you by 45 days, the alternates you name will receive the property he or she would have received.

> EXAMPLE: Christine is not married and has no children. She is very close to her sister Karen, and wants to leave all her property to her.
>
> In her will, Christine names Karen as her main beneficiary. As alternates, she names Karen's two children.

> EXAMPLE: Ari leaves all of his property to his two brothers Seth and David. Because Seth is more financially stable, he indicates that Seth should get one-quarter of his estate and David should get three-quarters. He names his cousin Rachel as an alternate beneficiary for David's share. She will get three-quarters of Ari's estate if David does not survive Ari. Ari names his favorite charity

as an alternate for Seth's share. If Seth does not survive Ari, the charity will get one-quarter of the estate.

If you like, you may also name a second level of alternates—that is, alternates to take the property should both your main and alternate beneficiaries not survive you by 45 days or more.

If you name more than one alternate beneficiary and one or more of them does not survive you, the surviving alternates will receive any property that would have gone to a deceased alternate.

If you name more than one alternate beneficiary but don't name any second alternates for those beneficiaries, the surviving alternate beneficiaries will share the property that any deceased beneficiary would have received.

> **EXAMPLE:** In her will, JoEllen leaves all her property to her partner, Katrine. She names her nephews, Jacob and Joseph, as alternates and does not name second alternates. When JoEllen dies, Katrine and Jacob have already passed away. Joseph inherits all of JoEllen's property.

Making a Different Plan

This option lets you create a whole new plan that takes effect only if your main beneficiary or beneficiaries do not survive you by 45 days. Your alternate plan—Plan B—can include as many specific bequests as you wish. (See "Making Specific Bequests," below.)

After you have made all your specific bequests, you can also name someone to take the rest of your property. This is called your residuary beneficiary. (See "Naming Residuary Beneficiaries," below.)

> **EXAMPLE:** Sven wants to leave all his property to Jeannette, his companion, if she's alive when he dies. But thinking about what he would want to happen if Jeannette were not around to get everything, he decides that he would want to divide his property among relatives and charities.

When he sits down with Quicken WillMaker to make his will, Sven names Jeannette to take all of his property. Then, when it's time to name alternates, he chooses the Plan B option and leaves $10,000 to a local food bank, his piano to his niece and everything else to his brother.

If You Do Not Name Alternates

If you leave your entire estate to one person or a group of people, you do not name alternate beneficiaries, and your primary beneficiaries do not survive you, then your estate will be distributed according to the laws of your state. (See "Dying Without a Will" in Chapter 1.)

Making Specific Bequests

This section discusses how to make specific bequests—that is, leave specific property items to specific people or groups. You should read this section if you:

- left most of your property to one or more main beneficiaries but want to leave some items to others
- want to divide your property among several beneficiaries, without leaving most or all of it to one or more main beneficiaries, or
- left everything to one or more beneficiaries, but instead of naming alternates for those beneficiaries, you want to make a Plan B to take effect if your main beneficiaries don't survive you.

Quicken WillMaker lets you make an unlimited number of separate specific bequests. For each one, you must provide this information:

- a description of the item—for example, a house, cash, an heirloom or a car
- the names of the people or organizations you want to get the items, and
- if you wish, the name of an alternate beneficiary, who will receive specific property if your first beneficiary does not survive you by 45 days. You can name more than one alternate beneficiary; if you do, you will also decide what share of the property each will receive.

Describing the Property

The first part of making a specific bequest is to describe the property you want to pass to a certain beneficiary or beneficiaries you have in mind. For example, if you want to leave your guitar to your best friend, you would begin by entering a brief description of the guitar, such as "my 1959 Martin guitar."

When describing an item, be as concise as you can, but use enough detail so that people will be able to identify and find the property. Most often, this will not be difficult: "my baby grand piano," "my collection of blue apothecary jars" or "my llama throw rug" are all the description you will need for tangible items that are easy to locate. If an item is very valuable or could be easily confused with other property, make sure you include identifying characteristics such as location, serial number, color or some other unique feature.

> **CAUTION**
>
> **Do not include property that will pass by other means.** Before describing the property you wish to leave in a specific bequest, take a moment to reflect on what property you are legally able to pass in your will. If you have already arranged to leave property outside your will by using legal devices, such as life insurance, pay-on-death bank accounts or living trusts, you usually should not include that property in a specific bequest. (See "Property You Should Not Include in Your Will" in Chapter 4.)

Naming Beneficiaries

The second step in making a specific bequest is to name one or more beneficiaries. If you have already entered the name of a beneficiary in the Contact List, select the name from the list and paste it in the beneficiary field. (See the Users' Manual for help.)

Beneficiaries' names need not be the names that appear on their birth certificates; as long as the names you use clearly identify the beneficiaries, all is well.

Tips on Describing Property in Your Will

Here is how to identify different types of property with enough detail to prevent confusion:

- **Household furnishings.** You normally need not get very specific, unless an object is particularly valuable. It is enough to list the location of the property: "all household furnishings and possessions in the apartment at 55 Drury Lane."
- **Real estate.** You can simply provide the street address or, for unimproved property, the name by which it is commonly known: "my condominium at 123 45th Avenue," "my summer home at 84 Memory Lane in Oakville" or "the vacant lot next to the McHenry Place on Old Farm Road." You do not need to provide the legal description from the deed.
- **Bank, stock and money market accounts.** List financial accounts by their account numbers. Also, include the name and location of the organization holding the property: "$20,000 from savings account #22222 at Independence Bank, Big Mountain, Idaho"; "my money market account #23456 at Beryl Pynch & Company, Chicago, Illinois"; or "100 shares of General Foods common stock."
- **Personal items.** As with household goods, it is usually adequate to briefly describe personal items and group them, unless they have significant monetary or sentimental value. For example, items of extremely valuable jewelry should normally be listed and identified separately, while a drawer full of costume jewelry and baubles could be grouped.

Do Not Place Conditions on Bequests

Don't place conditions on any of your bequests; it risks making a confusing and even unenforceable will.

Here are some examples of what not to do:

- "I leave my gold Rolex to Andres, but only if he divorces his current wife, Samantha." Such a bequest would not be considered legally valid, because it encourages the breakup of a family.
- "I leave my dental office equipment to Claude, as long as he sets up a dental practice in San Francisco." The reason this bequest is unwieldy becomes obvious once you think ahead to the need for constant supervision. Who would be responsible for tracking Claude's dentistry career and making sure he ends up in San Francisco? What if Claude initially practices in San Francisco, using the equipment he was willed, then moves to grow grapes in the Napa Valley? Must he give up the equipment? To whom?
- "I leave my vintage Barbie doll collection to Collette, if the dolls are still in good condition." Who is to judge whether the dolls are in good condition? What happens if they aren't?

SEE AN EXPERT

When to see a lawyer. If you are determined to place conditions on beneficiaries or property, consult a lawyer who is experienced in drafting bequests that will adequately address these potentially complex arrangements.

Minors or Young Adults

If any of the beneficiaries you name is a minor (under 18) or young adult (under 35), you will have a chance, in a later part of Quicken WillMaker, to choose someone to manage the property for them until they are older. (See Chapter 6.)

Multiple Beneficiaries

If you name two or more beneficiaries to share a specific bequest, you will later be asked to specify each person's share. To avoid possible tiffs among your beneficiaries, the property you plan to leave them either should be property that is easily divided or property that you intend to be sold so that the proceeds can be split. For property that requires discretion to divide it may be wiser to leave items separately.

Note for California Readers:
Be Cautious About Gifts to Caregivers

If you reside in California and want to leave a substantial gift to your caregiver, see a lawyer.

California law voids gifts to "care custodians" from "dependent adults." (Cal. Prob. Code § 21350.) This law aims to thwart caregivers from taking advantage of someone who depends on them. It does not apply to caregivers who are relatives. And for many estates (those larger than $100,000), the law invalidates only gifts over $3,000.

If you really want to leave a gift to a caregiver, you can. You'll need to see a lawyer, who can certify that the transfer is legitimate. Getting such an "independent certification" should eliminate any problems with the gift.

The law casts a very broad net and could easily invalidate gifts that you knowingly and freely intended to make. For example, a simple gift to a neighbor who brings meals and helps you pay bills could be voided, as could a large gift to a live-in caregiver who has also become a good friend.

It's likely that California will revise this law in the near future to reduce the likelihood that it will void genuine gifts. However, to be safe, consult a lawyer if you plan to leave a gift to a caregiver.

Organizations

You may want to leave property to a charity or a public or private organization—for example, the American Red Cross, the Greenview Battered Women's Shelter or the University of Illinois at Champaign-Urbana.

The organization you name need not be set up as a nonprofit, unless you wish your estate to qualify for a charitable estate tax deduction. (See Chapter 12.) It can be any organization you consider worthy of your bequest. The only limitation is that the organization must not be set up for some illicit or illegal purpose.

The organization you name will receive your gift with no strings attached. You cannot use your will to describe how the property should be used. If you want to do that—for example, if you want a gift to your alma mater to be used as a scholarship for a student who gets above a 3.5 grade point average—see an experienced estate planning attorney for advice.

When naming an organization, be sure to enter its complete name, which may be different from the truncated version by which it is commonly known. Several different organizations may use similar names—and you want to be sure your bequest goes to the one you have in mind. Someone at the organization will be more than happy to help you get it straight.

Specifying Shares

If you name a group of beneficiaries to receive specific property, Quicken WillMaker will ask you whether you want them to receive equal or unequal shares of the property. If you want it shared unequally, the shares must add up to one. Quicken WillMaker will warn you if your computations are off.

> **EXAMPLE:** Fred Wagner wants to leave an undeveloped real estate parcel to his three children, Mary, Sue and Peter. Because he has already paid for Mary's graduate school education, he wants to give Sue and Peter greater percentages of the property in case they

want to go back to school, too. He lists his children and the share of his property to which they are entitled this way: Mary Wagner (1/5), Susan Wagner (2/5) and Peter Wagner (2/5).

Naming Alternates

To receive property under your will, a beneficiary must survive you by 45 days. Quicken WillMaker assumes that if a beneficiary survives you by only a few days or weeks, you would prefer the property to pass to an alternate or residuary beneficiary named in your will, rather than have the property pass along with the beneficiary's other property.

With Quicken WillMaker, you can name one or more alternate beneficiaries to take the bequest if your first choices do not survive you by the required period.

> **EXAMPLE:** Joan leaves her horse to her brother Pierre. In case Pierre does not survive her by 45 days and so become eligible to receive this bequest, Joan names her sister Carmen as Pierre's alternate beneficiary.

If you name multiple beneficiaries to receive property, you can name an alternate for each beneficiary.

> **EXAMPLE:** Gideon leaves his house to his three nephews—Aaron, Thomas and Zeke—in equal shares. In case Aaron does not survive him by 45 days, Gideon specifies that the house should then go to the survivors, Thomas and Zeke. In case Thomas does not survive him by 45 days, Gideon names his brother Horace to take Thomas's share. In case Zeke does not survive him by 45 days, Gideon specifies that Aaron and Horace should take Zeke's share.

If you do not name alternates for specific bequests, and the primary beneficiary dies before you do, the property will become part of your residuary estate.

Reviewing Specific Bequests

When you complete a specific bequest—that is, you have identified the property, named the beneficiary and named an alternate beneficiary— Quicken WillMaker will display the beneficiary's name on the screen. You can also view this list by property. You can then add a new bequest or review, change or delete any of the bequests you have made.

Naming Residuary Beneficiaries

Quicken WillMaker will ask you to name a beneficiary for your residuary estate only if either of the following is true:

- You chose not to name one main beneficiary to receive most or all of your property.
- After leaving all your property to one beneficiary, you chose to create an alternate plan, or Plan B, in case your first choice does not survive you. In this case, you name a residuary beneficiary as part of your alternate plan.

If you left all or most of your property to one or more beneficiaries, they will receive property that does not pass in a specific bequest or by means other than your will. In effect, they will automatically become your residuary beneficiaries.

> **EXAMPLE:** When Mikki makes her will, she leaves all her property to her husband, Tyler. By the time she dies, 15 years later, she has acquired a new car, stocks and other items. Everything goes to her husband.

What a Residuary Beneficiary Receives

Your residuary beneficiary receives anything that does not go, for one reason or another, to the beneficiaries you named to receive specific bequests.

Specifically, the residuary beneficiary receives property that:

- you overlook when making your will
- you acquire after you make your will, and
- does not go to the person you named to get it in a specific bequest—for example, because that person died before you did and you did not name an alternate beneficiary, or the alternate also failed to survive you.

EXAMPLE: In her will, Sara, a widow, leaves many different items to many different beneficiaries: books to her daughter, jewelry to a friend, a car to her nephew and so on. She doesn't name alternate beneficiaries for these specific bequests, but she names her daughter as residuary beneficiary.

When Sara dies, some years after making the will, the friend to whom she left the jewelry has already died. The jewelry goes to Sara's daughter, as does the other property that Sara acquired since making her will.

There is no need to describe, in your will, the property the residuary beneficiary will receive. By definition, your residuary estate is the rest of your property that does not pass outside of your will or in a specific bequest, so it is impossible to know exactly what it will include. When your executor inventories your entire estate after your death, he or she will identify your residuary estate.

How to Name Residuary Beneficiaries

You can name one or more individuals or organizations, or a combination of both, as residuary beneficiaries. Use the Contact List to select and paste the name if it is already on the list. (See the Users' Manual for help.)

If you name more than one residuary beneficiary, Quicken WillMaker will ask you what shares you want each to receive.

EXAMPLE: After making a large number of specific bequests in his Quicken WillMaker will, Maurice leaves his residuary estate to his four children, Clara, Heinrich, Lise and Wiebke. He wants Lise and Wiebke each to receive 30% (3/10) of the property and the other two children to each receive 20% (2/10) each. So he indicates that he wants to leave the residuary estate in unequal shares and enters the desired shares on the screen provided for this purpose.

If any of the beneficiaries you name is a minor (under 18) or young adult (under 35), you will have a chance, in a later part of Quicken WillMaker, to choose someone to manage the property for them until they are older. (See Chapter 6.)

Naming Alternates

Quicken WillMaker also asks you to choose an alternate residuary beneficiary, in case your first choice does not survive you by 45 days.

If you do not name alternates for specific bequests, and the primary beneficiary dies before you do, the property will become part of your residuary estate.

> **CAUTION**
>
> **When you need not bother naming alternates.** You do not have to name an alternate residuary beneficiary, and not everyone is concerned about this issue. Younger people in reasonably good health are usually confident that they can address a beneficiary's premature death by updating their wills. However, many married people are concerned about what will happen if they die close together in time. And older people in poor health may fear that they won't have an opportunity to update their wills if their first choice beneficiaries die before they do.

> **EXAMPLE:** After making many specific bequests, Alfredo leaves his residuary estate to his daughter, Vanessa. He then specifies that if Vanessa does not survive him, her share should go to her two children—Alfredo's grandchildren. If Vanessa does not survive

Alfredo, and Alfredo does not write a new will, Vanessa's children would each take one-half of Alfredo's residuary estate.

EXAMPLE: Jack makes a large number of specific bequests to friends and relatives and then leaves his residuary estate to his friend, Joe. He names another friend, Josette, as alternate residuary beneficiary. Josette will be entitled to take property under Jack's will only if Joe does not survive Jack by 45 days and there is property left over after the specific bequests are distributed.

Naming a Trust as Beneficiary

If you like, you can also name a trust as a beneficiary of your will. When you die, the property you leave will be transferred to the trust, rather than directly to a person or organization.

Leaving property to a living trust with a pour-over will. If you have a living trust, you can use your will to transfer property to the trust after your death. If the primary purpose of your will is to funnel property to a living trust, the will is called a "pour-over" will.

Making a pour-over will means you don't have to transfer every minor asset into your living trust. Also, if you name your trust as the sole beneficiary or the residuary beneficiary of your will, the pour-over will covers any property that you might have neglected to transfer to the trust during your life.

But there's one important thing to keep in mind when you make a pour-over will: The property you leave through the will may have to go through probate when you die. Because living trusts are designed to avoid probate, if you leave too much property through your will, you may end up thwarting your own best intentions.

Most people who make a pour-over will leave most or all of their property through the living trust or through other beneficiary designations (such as life insurance), so that very little property ends up passing through the will. Whatever approach you take, before you make a pour-over will, be sure you know how much property your state allows you to pass through your will without triggering probate proceedings. (For more information about probate and how to avoid it, see Chapter 12.)

To leave property to your living trust, name your trust as beneficiary for that property, using the trustee's name and the name of the trust. For example: "John Doe as trustee of the John Doe Living Trust, dated January 1, 20xx."

Leaving property to a special needs trust. Special needs trusts allow people with disabilities to receive additional support without risking their eligibility for government benefits. Money or property given directly to people with disabilities is likely to interfere with their ability to receive disability benefits. For this reason, if a loved one has a special needs trust, you may want to name that trust as a beneficiary of your will. To do so, enter the name of the trustee and the full legal name of the trust as beneficiary. Example: "James Leung as the trustee of the The Eric Workman Special Needs Trust".

Providing Management for Children's Property

Except for items of little value, minors are not permitted by law to receive property directly. This legal rule is most important if the property is:

- cash or other liquid assets—for example, a savings account that can easily be spent, or
- property that comes with a title document—for example, real estate.

Instead, that property will have to be distributed to and managed by a responsible adult. It is of vital importance to both your own children and any other young beneficiaries that you arrange for this management yourself, in your will. If you don't, a court may need to appoint and supervise someone—an expensive and time-consuming alternative. It's better to make your own choice and state it in your will, instead of leaving the decision to someone else.

TIP

Keeping track of children's property. The person you name to take care of your child's property will need access to financial records related to property that the child will own. For help collecting this information, use Quicken WillMaker's Information for Caregivers and Survivors form.

Property management consists of naming a trusted adult to care for and accurately account for a young person's property until the minor turns a specific age. The property being managed must be held, invested or spent in the best interest of the minor. In other words, someone other than the young person will decide if his or her inheritance will be spent on college tuition or a new sports car.

Quicken WillMaker enables you to establish management for two types of property:

- property that passes to minors under your will (they do not have to be your own children), and
- property that passes to your minor children outside of your will.

For property received under your will, this management may last until the minor turns an age you choose. For property that your minor children receive outside of your will, the management provided by Quicken WillMaker lasts until the children become adults—18 years old in most states.

Explaining Your Bequests to Your Children

Using Quicken WillMaker, you are free to divide your property among your children as you see fit. If your children are already responsible adults, your prime concern will likely be fairness—given the circumstances and the children's needs. Often, this will mean dividing your property equally among your children. Sometimes, however, the special health or educational needs of one child, the relative affluence and stability of another or the fact that you are estranged from a child will be the impetus for you to divide the property unevenly.

Doing this can sometimes raise serious angst; a child who receives less property may conclude that you cared for him or her less. To clear up confusion, you may wish to explain your choices. Because of the risk of adding illegal or confusing language, Quicken WillMaker does not allow you to make this explanation in your will. Fortunately, there is a sound and sensible way to express your reasons and feelings. Simply prepare a separate letter to accompany your will. (See Chapter 11.)

What Happens If the Minor Does Not Get Property

If you arrange for property management for a minor, but the minor never actually becomes entitled to the property, no harm is done. The management provisions for that minor are ignored. For instance, suppose you identify a favorite niece to take property as an alternate beneficiary and provide management for that property until the niece turns 25. If the niece never gets to take the property because your first-choice beneficiary survives you, no property management will be established for her, since none will be needed.

Property Management for Property That Passes Under Your Will

Quicken WillMaker offers three approaches to property management for property that passes to minors under your will:

- the Uniform Transfers to Minors Act—for property left in your will—in all states except South Carolina and Vermont
- the Quicken WillMaker child's trust—for property left in your will—as an alternative to the UTMA and as an option for will makers who live in one of the two states that have not adopted the UTMA, and
- the Quicken WillMaker pot trust—for property left to your children in your will—if at least one of your children is younger than 25 years old.

The Uniform Transfers to Minors Act

The Uniform Transfers to Minors Act (UTMA) allows you to name a custodian to manage property you leave to a minor. The management ends when the minor reaches age 18 to 25, depending on state law.

States are free to adopt or reject the UTMA, which is a model law proposed by a group of legal scholars. All but two states have adopted the UTMA, many making minor changes to it. It is likely that the UTMA will be universally adopted in a few more years.

If the UTMA has been adopted in your state, you may use it to specify a custodian to manage property you leave to a minor in your will until the age at which the laws of your state require that it be turned over to the minor. Depending on your state, this varies from 18 to 25. Quicken WillMaker keeps track of the state you indicate as your residence and tells you whether the UTMA is available and, if so, the age at which property management under it must end.

Age Limits for Property Management in UTMA States

State	Age at Which Minor Gets Property	State	Age at Which Minor Gets Property
Alabama	21	Missouri	21
Alaska	18 to 25	Montana	21
Arizona	21	Nebraska	21
Arkansas	18 to 21	Nevada	18 to 25
California	18 to 25	New Hampshire	21
Colorado	21	New Jersey	18 to 21
Connecticut	21	New Mexico	21
Delaware	21	New York	21
District of Columbia	18 to 21	North Carolina	18 to 21
Florida	21	North Dakota	21
Georgia	21	Ohio	18 to 21
Hawaii	21	Oklahoma	18 to 21
Idaho	21	Oregon	21 to 25
Illinois	21	Pennsylvania	21 to 25
Indiana	21	Rhode Island	21
Iowa	21	South Dakota	18
Kansas	21	Tennessee	21 to 25
Kentucky	18	Texas	21
Maine	18 to 21	Utah	21
Maryland	21	Virginia	18 to 21
Massachusetts	21	Washington	21
Michigan	18 to 21	West Virginia	21
Minnesota	21	Wisconsin	21
Mississippi	21	Wyoming	21

States That Have Not Adopted the UTMA

The UTMA has not been adopted in South Carolina or Vermont.

If you are a resident of one of these states, you can set up property management for any minor or young adult beneficiary using the Quicken WillMaker child's trust, discussed below. If you have two or more children and at least one of them is under 25 years old, you may also use the Quicken WillMaker pot trust, discussed below.

Among the powers the UTMA gives the custodian are the rights to collect, hold, manage, invest and reinvest the property and to spend it "for the use and benefit of the minor." All of these actions can be taken without getting approval from a court. The custodian must also keep records so that tax returns can be filed on behalf of the minor and must otherwise act prudently in controlling the property.

Special Rule for Life Insurance

Often the major source of property left to children comes from a life insurance policy naming the children as beneficiaries. If you want the insurance proceeds for a particular child to be managed, and you live in a state that has adopted the UTMA, instruct your insurance agent to provide you with the form necessary to name a custodian to manage the property for the beneficiary under the terms of this Act.

The Quicken WillMaker Child's Trust

The Quicken WillMaker child's trust, which can be used in all states, is a legal structure you establish in your will. If you create a trust, any property a minor beneficiary gets will be managed by a person or institution you choose to serve as trustee until the beneficiary turns an age you choose—through age 35. The trustee's powers are listed in your will. The trustee may use trust assets for the education, medical needs and living expenses of the beneficiary. All property you leave to a beneficiary for whom a trust is established will be managed under the terms of the trust.

Because management under the Quicken WillMaker child's trust can be extended through age 35, it is also suitable to use for property left to young adults. (The pros and cons of management options are discussed in "Choosing Among Management Options," below.)

The Quicken WillMaker Pot Trust

The Quicken WillMaker pot trust is a legal structure you can establish in your will. However, instead of creating a separate child's trust for the property you leave to each child, you create one trust for all the property you leave to your children. You name a single trustee to manage the property for the benefit of the children as a group, without regard to how much is spent on an individual child.

For example, if there are three children and one of them needs an expensive medical procedure, all of the property could be spent on that child, even though the other children would receive nothing. While this potential result may seem unfair, it in fact mirrors the reality faced by many families: Some children need more money than others.

The pot trust will last until the youngest child turns an age you specify up to age 25. If there is a significant age gap between your children, the oldest children may have to wait many years past the time they become adults before they receive their shares of the property. For instance, if one of your children is five and another child is 17—and you specify that the pot trust should end when the youngest turns 18—the 17-year-old will have to wait at least until age 30 to receive a share of the property left in the trust.

> CAUTION
>
> **All or none must go in the pot.** The Quicken WillMaker pot trust option is available only for property you leave to all of your children as a group. If you want to use the pot trust for some but not all of your children, you will need to see a lawyer. (See Chapter 13.)

When Will Property Management End?

The age at which property management ends depends on the type of management you select.

- **UTMA.** State law determines when property management ends. In some states, you may choose from a limited age range. See "The Uniform Transfers to Minors Act," above.
- **Quicken WillMaker child's trust.** The trust ends when the child turns an age you choose, up to age 35.
- **Quicken WillMaker pot trust.** The trust ends when your youngest child turns an age you choose, up to age 25.
- **Other property management.** Property management for property your child receives outside of your will ends when the child becomes a legal adult—age 18 in most states.

Choosing Among Management Options

For each minor or young adult to whom you leave property in your will, you must decide which management approach to use: the UTMA, a child's trust or the pot trust. This section helps you decide which is best.

SEE AN EXPERT

Needs not covered by Quicken WillMaker. The property management features offered by Quicken WillMaker—the UTMA, child's trust and pot trust—provide the property manager with broad management authority adequate for most minors and young adults. However, they are not designed to:

- provide skilled long-term management of a business
- provide for management of funds beyond age 35 for a person with spendthrift tendencies or other personal habits that may impede sound financial management beyond young adulthood, or
- meet the special needs of beneficiaries who have disabilities. A physical, mental or developmental disability will likely require management

customized to the beneficiary's circumstances, both to perpetuate the beneficiary's way of life and to preserve the property, while assuring that the beneficiary continues to qualify for government benefits.

To learn more about preparing trusts for people with disabilities, read *Special Needs Trusts* (Nolo), by Stephen Elias. For other situations described here, consult an experienced estate planning attorney. (See Chapter 13.)

Using the UTMA

As a general rule, the less valuable the property involved and the more mature the child, the more appropriate the UTMA is, because it is simpler to use than a child's trust or pot trust. There are a couple of reasons for this.

Because the UTMA is built into state law, banks, insurance companies, brokerage firms and other financial institutions know about it, so it should be easy for the custodian to carry out property management duties. To set up a child's trust or pot trust, the financial institution would have to be given a copy of the trust document and may tie up the proceeding in red tape to be sure the trustee is acting under its terms.

Also, a custodian acting under the UTMA need not file a separate income tax return for the property being managed; it can be included in the young beneficiary's return. However, in a child's trust or a pot trust, both the beneficiary and the trust must file returns.

Because the UTMA requires that management end at a relatively young age, if the property you are leaving is worth $100,000 or less—or if the child is likely to be able to handle more than that by age 21 (25 in Alaska, California, Nevada, Oregon, Pennsylvania or Tennessee)— use the UTMA. After all, $100,000 is likely to be used up before management under the UTMA ends.

Using the Quicken WillMaker Child's Trust

Generally, the more property is worth, and the less mature the young beneficiary, the better it is to use the child's trust, even though doing so creates more work for the property manager than does the UTMA.

For example, in a child's trust, the property manager must keep the beneficiary informed, manage trust assets prudently (meeting the requirements of state law) and file a separate tax return for the trust each year.

However, if a minor or young adult stands to get a fairly large amount of property—such as $200,000 or more—you might not want it all distributed by your state's UTMA cutoff age, which is usually 18 or 21. In such circumstances, you may be better off using the Quicken WillMaker child's trust. Under the child's trust, management can last until an age you choose, to age 35.

Choosing an age for a particular beneficiary to get whatever trust property has not been spent on the beneficiary's needs will depend on:

- the amount of money or other property involved
- how much control you would like to impose over it
- the beneficiary's likely level of maturity as a young adult (for small children, this may be difficult to predict, but by the time youngsters reach their teens, you should have a pretty good indication), and
- whether the property you leave, such as rental property or a small business, needs sophisticated management that a young beneficiary is unlikely to master.

Using the Quicken WillMaker Pot Trust

As a general rule, the pot trust makes sense only when you have two or more children and they are young and fairly close in age. For instance, if one of your children is 20 and another child of a later marriage is two, and you specify that the pot trust should end when the younger child turns 18, the 20-year-old would have to wait until age 36 to receive the property. However, the pot trust option is available to you as long as any of your children is under age 25.

Like the trustee of a child's trust, a pot trust trustee must invest trust assets following the rules set out in state law, communicate regularly with the trust beneficiaries to keep them informed and file annual tax returns. The trustee of the pot trust also has the significant added responsibility of weighing competing claims from the children when deciding how to spend trust assets.

Property Management for Property That Does Not Pass Under Your Will

The UTMA, Quicken WillMaker child's trust and pot trust are good management options for property that minor or young adult beneficiaries receive under your will. However, if you have minor children and they receive property of significant value outside of your will, a court will usually have to step in and appoint a guardian to manage the property under court supervision until the children turn 18.

The two most common ways that children receive property outside of a will are from life insurance or through a living trust. (See Chapter 12.) While it is possible to provide for management of this type of property through your life insurance agent under the UTMA or within the living trust itself, often no such management is established and a property guardianship is required.

In addition, property that your children receive from other sources—the lottery, a gift from an aunt or uncle, or earnings from playing in a rock band—may also need to be managed by a property guardian.

It is always better to specify who will be managing any such property that your minor children come to own. Otherwise, the court will appoint someone who may or may not have your children's best interests in mind. If you are using the Quicken WillMaker child's trust, a pot trust or the UTMA to provide management for property you are leaving to your children in your will, the person you have named as trustee or custodian would also be a good choice for property guardian. Another possible choice is the person you chose to be personal guardian, if you think he or she will handle the property wisely for the benefit of the minor. You also may wish to choose someone else entirely. Next, we offer some tips to help you pick the right person.

Naming a Property Manager

You may name one person to manage the property of a minor. You can also name one alternate (sometimes called "successor"), who will take over if your first choice is unable to serve.

Choosing a property manager is an important decision. Name someone you trust, who is familiar with property management and who shares your attitudes and values about how the money should be spent.

> **CAUTION**
>
> **Parents do not get the job automatically.** You may be surprised to learn that the child's other parent probably will not be able to automatically step in and handle property you leave your children in your will. Rather, unless you provide for management in your will, that other parent usually will have to petition the court to be appointed as the property manager and then handle the property under court supervision until the children turn 18. So, if you want your children's other parent to manage the property you are leaving your children, name that person to manage your children's property.
>
> Keep in mind that you can only name the other parent as custodian or trustee if there is a chance that the other parent will be alive when the child receives the gift. For example, if you leave a gift to the other parent and you name the child as alternate for that gift, you cannot name the other parent to be trustee or custodian of that gift because the child would only receive the property if the other parent is not alive.

Whomever you choose, it is essential to get his or her consent first. This will also give you a chance to discuss, in general terms, how you would like the property to be managed to be sure the manager you select agrees with your vision and fully understands the beneficiary's needs.

The next sections offer tips on choosing the right property manager. In most situations, a trusted adult will be the best choice, but in some rare cases, you may want to name an institution, such as a bank.

Choosing a Property Manager

As a general rule, name a trusted adult who lives in or near to the state where the property will be managed—or is at least be willing to travel there if needed.

You need not worry about finding a financial wizard to be your property manager because that person will have the power to hire professionals to prepare accountings and tax returns and to give investment advice. Anyone hired for such help may be paid out of the property being managed. The main job is to manage the property honestly, make basic decisions about how to take care of the assets wisely and sensibly mete out the money to the trust beneficiary.

It is usually preferable to combine the personal care and property management functions for a particular minor child in the hands of one person. Think first who is likely to be caring for the children if you die, and then consider whether that person is also a good choice for property manager. If you must name two different people, try to choose people who get along well; they will have to work together.

If you believe that the person who will be caring for the minor is not the best person to handle the minor's finances, consider another adult who is capable and is willing to serve.

For property you leave to young adults who are too old to have a person guardian, select an honest person with business savvy to manage the property.

> **EXAMPLE:** Orenthal and Ariadne agree that Ariadne's sister, Penny, should be guardian of their kids should they both die, but that the $200,000 worth of stock the three kids will inherit might better be handled by someone with more business experience and who will be better able to resist the children's urgings to spend the money frivolously. In each of their wills, they name Penny as personal guardian of the children, but also create trusts for the property they are leaving to their children. They name each other as trustees, and Orenthal's mother, Phyllis, who has investment and business knowledge and lots of experience in

handling headstrong adolescents, as the alternate trustee, after obtaining her consent. Orenthal and Ariadne also decide that one of their children, who is somewhat immature, should receive his share of the estate—at least the portion not already disbursed for his benefit by the trustee—upon turning 25, and the other two children should get their shares when they turn 21.

Selecting an Institution as Trustee

If you are using the UTMA, you must name a person as custodian; you cannot name an institution. If you're creating a trust, you can name an institution to serve as trustee, but it is rarely a good idea. Most banks will not accept a trust with less than several hundred thousand dollars' worth of liquid assets.

When banks do agree to take a trust, they charge large management and administrative fees. All trustees are entitled to reasonable compensation for their services—paid from trust assets. But family members or close friends who act as trustees often waive payments or accept far less than banks. If you cannot find an individual you think is suitable for handling your assets and do not have enough property to be managed by a financial institution, you may be better off not creating a trust.

Also, it is common for banks to manage the assets of all trusts worth less than $1 million as part of one large fund, while charging fees as if they were individually managed. Any noninstitutional trustee who invests trust money in a conservatively run mutual fund can normally do at least as well at a fraction of the cost.

Examples of Property Management

Here are some examples of how the Quicken WillMaker property management options might be selected. The following scenarios are only intended as suggestions. Remember, if you live in South Carolina or Vermont, you cannot create an UTMA custodianship.

EXAMPLE: **Married, adult children age 25 and older.** You want to leave all your property, worth $250,000, to your spouse and name surviving children as alternate beneficiaries. As long as you think the children are all sufficiently mature to handle their shares of the property if your spouse does not survive you, answer no when Quicken WillMaker asks if you wish to set up property management.

EXAMPLE: **Married, children aged 2, 5 and 9.** You want to leave all your property, which is worth $250,000, to your spouse and name your children as alternate beneficiaries. You use the property management feature and select the UTMA option to manage the property if it passes to your children. You name your wife's mother—the same person you have named as personal guardian—as custodian, and name your brother as alternate personal guardian and alternate custodian. The property will be managed by the custodian until the age set by your state's law.

You also name your wife's mother as property guardian if management is needed for property your minor children receive outside of your will.

Later, when your children are older and you have accumulated more property, you may wish to make a new will and switch from the UTMA management approach to a pot trust so that the property can be used to meet the children's needs as required.

EXAMPLE: **Single or married; two minor children from a previous marriage and one minor child with your present partner.** You want to leave all your property, which is worth $250,000, directly to your children. You can use the UTMA, set up the trust for each child or create a pot trust. You should also name a property guardian to manage any property your minor child might get outside of your will.

> ⚠ CAUTION
>
> **Beware property rights of spouses and domestic partners.** If you are married or in a registered domestic partnership, your spouse or partner may have a right to claim a portion of your property, so it is usually unwise to leave it all to your children unless your spouse or partner agrees with that plan. (See "Property Ownership Rules for Married People" in Chapter 4.)

EXAMPLE: **Single or married; two adult children from a previous marriage—ages 23 and 27—and one minor child with your present partner.** You decide to divide $300,000 equally among the children. To accomplish this, you establish a trust for each child from the previous marriage and put the termination age at 30. You name your current spouse, who gets along well with the children, as trustee and a local trust company as alternate trustee. Because your third child is an unusually mature teenager, you choose the UTMA for this child and select 21 as the age at which this child takes any remaining property outright. You appoint your wife as custodian and your sister as successor custodian.

EXAMPLE: **Married or single; one daughter, age 32, and three minor grandchildren.** You want to leave $50,000 directly to each of the grandchildren. You establish a custodianship under the UTMA for each grandchild and name your daughter as custodian and her husband as successor custodian.

Choosing an Executor

Y ou should name an executor to wrap up your will. After your
death, that person will have legal responsibility for safeguarding
and handling your property, seeing that debts and taxes are paid
and distributing what is left to your beneficiaries as your will directs.

Executor or Personal Representative?		
The following states use the term "personal representative" instead of "executor," but it means the same thing. If you live in one of these states, you will see the term "personal representative" in your will.		
Alabama	Idaho	New Mexico
Alaska	Maine	North Dakota
Arizona	Michigan	South Carolina
Colorado	Minnesota	South Dakota
Florida	Montana	Utah
Hawaii	Nebraska	Wisconsin

TIP
Make your will and records accessible. You can help with the
executor's first task: locating your will. Keep the original in a fairly obvious place—
such as a desk or file cabinet. And make sure your executor has access to it.

Duties of an Executor

Serving as an executor can be fairly easy, or it can require a good deal of
time and patience—depending on the amount of property involved and
the complexity of the plans for it.

The Executor's Job

Your executor will have a number of duties, most of which do not require special expertise and can usually be accomplished without outside help. An executor typically must:
- obtain certified copies of the death certificate
- locate will beneficiaries
- examine and inventory the deceased person's safe deposit boxes
- collect the deceased person's mail
- cancel credit cards and subscriptions
- notify Social Security and other benefit plan administrators of the death
- learn about the deceased person's property—which may involve examining bankbooks, deeds, insurance policies, tax returns and many other records
- get bank accounts released or, in the case of pay-on-death accounts, get them transferred to their new owner, and
- collect any death benefits from life insurance policies, Social Security, veterans benefits and other benefits due from the deceased's union, fraternal society or employer.

In addition to these mundane tasks, the executor will typically have to:
- file papers in court to start the probate process and obtain the necessary authority to act as executor
- handle the probate court process—which involves transferring property and making sure the deceased's final debts and taxes are paid, and
- prepare final income tax forms for the deceased and, if necessary, file estate tax returns for the estate.

Note for Texas Residents: Independent Administration

Like many states, Texas offers a simplified probate process. In the Lone Star State, it's called "independent administration" and it gives an executor broad powers to act without supervision of the probate court. For example, an independent executor can pay final bills and distribute property without the court's oversight.

Unlike other states, Texas requires a will to contain a bit of special language to request this simplified process. That's why your Quicken WillMaker will refers to your executor as your "independent executor" and includes the required language that permits the independent administration of your estate.

> **SEE AN EXPERT**
>
> **When to see a lawyer.** We've designed your will to request independent administration because it saves money and speeds up probate. If you want your executor to work under the close supervision of a court, see an experienced estate planning attorney for advice.

For these tasks, it may be necessary to hire outside professionals who will be paid out of the estate's assets—a lawyer to initiate and handle the probate process and an accountant to prepare the necessary tax forms. But in some states, because of simplified court procedures and adequate self-help law materials, even these tasks can be accomplished without outside assistance.

For help with the task of educating your executor, you can print out a document titled Letter to Executor, which you can give to the person you name to serve. The document offers guidance on the executor's duties.

RESOURCE

More help for executors. For a complete guide to an executor's duties and details about how to wrap up an estate, see *The Executor's Guide: Settling a Loved One's Estate or Trust,* by Mary Randolph (Nolo).

Posting a Bond

Sometimes, a probate court asks an executor to post a bond—an insurance policy that protects beneficiaries if the executor is dishonest or incompetent. Some probate courts require bonds for all executors, while others only require bonds for out-of-state executors. However, many courts won't demand a bond if the will says that no bond is required.

The will you make with Quicken WillMaker expressly states that no bond is necessary. As long as you choose an executor you trust, there's no reason your executor should have to go to the trouble of putting up a bond. Furthermore, the cost of the bond—usually about 10% of its face amount—comes out of your estate, so your beneficiaries receive less than they would if no bond was purchased.

SEE AN EXPERT

If you want to require a bond. If you're less than confident about your executor's competence or you feel that the extra insurance of a bond is worth the cost, see an experienced estate planning attorney who can draft your will to require your executor to post a bond.

Getting Paid

The laws of every state provide that an executor may be paid out of the estate. Depending on your state law, this payment may be:

- based on what the court considers reasonable
- a small percentage of the gross or net value of the estate, or
- set according to factors specified in your state's statutes.

An executor who either stands to get a large portion of the estate or is a close family relative, commonly does the work without being paid. Some will makers opt to leave their executors a specific bequest of money in appreciation for serving.

However, outside experts will almost always be paid out of the estate. The amount experts—including lawyers—are paid is totally under the control of the executor. However, a few states set out fees that may be charged by lawyers and other professionals—usually a percentage of the value of the estate.

> (!) CAUTION
>
> **Beware of lawyers' fees.** Lawyers commonly imply that the fee allowed by statute is the fee that they are required to charge for their services. In fact, lawyers are perfectly free to charge by the hour or to set a flat fee that is unrelated to the size of the estate. One of the most important tasks that your executor can perform is to negotiate a reasonable fee with any lawyer he or she may pick to help probate your estate. Be sure you explain this to your choice for executor.

Naming an Executor

Glancing through the list of the executor's duties mentioned above should tip you off about who might be the best person for the job. The prime characteristics are honesty, skill at organizing and finesse in keeping track of details. For many tasks, such as collecting mail and finding important records and papers, it may be most helpful to name someone who lives nearby or who is familiar with your business matters.

Choosing Your Executor

The most important guideline in naming an executor is to choose someone you trust enough to have access to your personal records and finances after your death. Many people choose someone who is also named to get a substantial amount of property under the will. This is sensible, because a person with an interest in how your property is distributed—a spouse, partner, child or close family member—is also likely to do a conscientious job as executor. And he or she will probably also come equipped with knowledge of where your records are kept and an understanding of why you want your property split up as you have directed.

Following are a few more things you may want to consider when making your choice. Whomever you choose, make sure the person you select is willing to do the job. Discuss the possible duties involved with your choice for executor before naming him or her in your will.

Naming Someone Who Lives Out of State

As a practical matter, it's wise to name an executor who lives close to you. It will be more difficult for the executor to handle day-to-day matters from a distance. But if the best person for the job lives far away, there's no law against naming that person in your will. Every state allows out-of-state executors to serve, though most states impose special rules on them. The table below sets out the details.

Naming More Than One Person

While you may name two executors to serve together, doing so is often not wise. Joint executors may act without each other's consent—and if they ever disagree, your estate may be the loser because of lengthy probate delays and court costs.

Naming an Institution

While it is almost always best to choose a trusted person for the job, you may not know anyone who is up to the task of winding up your estate—especially if your estate is large and complicated and your beneficiaries are either very old, very young or just inexperienced in financial matters. If so, you can select a professional management firm to act as your executor. (Banks often provide this service.)

If you are considering naming an institution as executor, be sure the one you choose is willing to act. Most will not accept the job unless your estate is fairly large. Also, institutions charge a hefty fee for acting as executor. They may charge both a percentage of the value of property to be managed and a number of smaller fees for routine services such as buying and selling property.

If You Do Not Name an Executor

If you do not name an executor in your will, the document will still be valid. But your decision will not have been a wise one. It will most often mean that a court will have to scurry to come up with a willing relative to serve. If that fails, the court will probably appoint someone to do the job who is likely to be unfamiliar with you, your property and your beneficiaries. People appointed by the court to serve are usually called administrators.

The laws in many states provide that anyone who is entitled under the will to take over half a person's property has first priority to serve as executor. If no such person is apparent, courts will generally look for someone to serve among the following groups of people, in the following order:

- surviving spouse or registered domestic partner
- children
- grandchildren
- great-grandchildren
- parents
- brothers and sisters
- grandparents
- uncles, aunts, first cousins
- children of a deceased spouse or partner
- other next of kin
- relatives of a deceased spouse or partner
- conservator or guardian
- public administrator
- creditors, and
- any other person.

Restrictions on Out-of-State Executors	
Alabama	Nonresident can be appointed executor only if already serving as executor of same estate in another state. (Ala. Code § 43-2-22)
Arkansas	Nonresident executor must appoint an in-state agent to accept legal papers. (Ark. Code Ann. § 28-48-101(b)(6))
Connecticut	Nonresident executor must appoint in-state probate court judge as agent to accept legal papers. (Conn. Gen. Stat. Ann. § 52-60)
Delaware	Nonresident executor must appoint county Register of Wills as the agent to accept legal papers. (Del. Code Ann. Tit. 12, § 1506)
District of Columbia	Nonresident executor must publish notices in a newspaper and appoint the probate register as agent to accept legal papers. (D.C. Code Ann. §§ 20-303, 20-343)
Florida	Nonresident can be appointed executor only if he or she is related by blood, marriage or adoption to person making will. (Fla. Stat. Ann. § 733.304)
Illinois	Nonresident executor may be required to post bond, even if will expressly states bond not required. (755 Ill. Comp. Stat. § 5/6-13)
Indiana	Nonresident can serve as executor if resident appointed coexecutor and nonresident posts a bond. Nonresident can serve alone if he or she posts a bond, files a written notice of acceptance and appoints an in-state agent to accept legal papers. (Ind. Code Ann. § 29-1-10-1)
Iowa	Nonresident can serve as executor only if resident appointed coexecutor, unless court allows nonresident to serve alone. (Iowa Code § 633.64)
Kansas	Nonresident executor must appoint an in-state agent to accept legal papers. (Kan. Stat. Ann. § 59-1706)
Kentucky	Nonresident can be appointed executor only if he or she is related by blood, marriage or adoption to person making will. (Ky. Rev. Stat. Ann. § 395.005)

Restrictions on Out-of-State Executors (continued)

Maryland	Nonresident executor must publish notices in a newspaper and appoint an in-state agent to accept legal papers. (Md. Code Ann. [Est. & Trusts]. §§ 5-105, 5-503)
Massachusetts	Nonresident executor must appoint an in-state agent to accept legal papers. (Mass. Gen. Laws ch. 195, § 8)
Missouri	Nonresident executor must appoint an in-state agent to accept legal papers. (Mo. Rev. Stat. § 473.117)
Nevada	Nonresident can serve as executor only if resident appointed coexecutor. (Nev. Rev. Stat. Ann. § 139.010)
New Hampshire	Nonresident executor must be approved by probate judge and must appoint an in-state agent to accept legal papers. (N.H. Stat. §§ 553:5, 553:25)
New Jersey	Nonresident must post bond unless will waives the requirement. (N.J. Stat. Ann. § 3B:15-1)
North Carolina	Nonresident executor must appoint an in-state agent to accept legal papers. (N.C. Gen. Stat. § 28A-4-2)
Ohio	Nonresident can be appointed executor only if he or she is related by blood, marriage or adoption to person making will—or if he or she lives in a state that permits nonresidents to serve. (Ohio Rev. Code Ann. § 2109.21)
Oklahoma	Nonresident executor must appoint an in-state agent to accept legal papers. (Okla. Stat. Ann. tit. 58, § 162)
Pennsylvania	Nonresident can serve as executor only with permission of register of wills. Nonresident executor must file an affidavit stating that estate has no known debts in Pennsylvania, and that he or she will not perform any duties prohibited in home state. (20 Pa. Cons. Stat. Ann. §§ 3157, 4101)
Rhode Island	Nonresident executor must be approved by a judge and must appoint an in-state agent to accept legal papers. (R.I. Gen. Laws §§ 33-8-7, 33-18-9)

Restrictions on Out-of-State Executors (continued)	
Tennessee	Nonresident executor must appoint secretary of state as agent to accept legal papers and may be required to post bond. Nonresident can also serve if resident appointed coexecutor. (Tenn. Code Ann. § 35-50-107)
Texas	Nonresident executor must appoint an in-state agent to accept legal papers. (Tex. Prob. Code Ann. § 78)
Vermont	Nonresident executor must appoint an in-state agent to accept legal papers. Nonresident executor can be appointed only with court approval; court must approve nonresident executor upon request of surviving spouse or civil union partner, adult children or parents or guardians of minor children. (Vt. Stat. Ann. tit. 14, § 904)
Virginia	Nonresident executor must post a bond and appoint an in-state agent to accept legal papers. Bond without a guarantee is permitted. (Va. Code Ann. § 26-59)
Washington	Nonresident executor must post a bond and appoint an in-state agent to accept legal papers. If nonresident is surviving spouse and sole beneficiary of will, or if will expressly states so, bond is not required. (Wash. Rev. Code Ann. §§ 11.28.185, 11.36.010)
West Virginia	Nonresident executor may serve if clerk of the county commission of the county where the probate is conducted serves as nonresident's agent. Nonresident must post bond unless will says otherwise. (W.Va. Code Ann. § 44-5-3)
Wisconsin	Nonresident executor must appoint an in-state agent to accept legal papers. At court's discretion, nonresident executor can be removed or refused appointment solely on grounds of residency. (Wis. Stat. Ann. § 856.23)
Wyoming	Nonresident executor must appoint an in-state agent to accept legal papers. (Wyo. Stat. § 2-11-301)

Naming an Alternate

In case you name someone to serve as executor who dies before you do or for any other reason cannot take on the responsibilities, you should name an alternate to serve instead.

- If you name coexecutors, your alternate executor will serve only if both coexecutors are unavailable.
- You may name up to two alternate executors. However, only one of them may serve at a time. Your second alternate will serve only if your executor(s) and your first alternate become unavailable.

EXAMPLE: Marsha names Bill and Jane as her coexecutors. She then names Susan as first alternate and Keith as second alternate. When Marsha dies, if either Bill or Jane is unavailable to be the executor of her estate, the other will serve alone. If both Bill and Jane are unavailable, Susan will serve. In the unlikely event that Bill, Jane and Susan are all unavailable, it will be up to Keith to wrap up Marsha's estate.

In choosing an alternate executor, consider the same factors you did in naming your first choice. (See "Choosing Your Executor," above.)

Debts, Expenses and Taxes

Money matters have a way of living on—even after your death. But you can easily guide your survivors through the vexing process of dealing with your debts and expenses by including clear instructions in your will.

In your will, you can:

- forgive debts that others owed you during your lifetime
- designate what property should be used to pay debts you owe at death, and
- designate what property should be used to pay state and federal death taxes owed by your estate or due on the property in it.

> **TIP**
>
> **Keeping track of your debts, expenses and taxes.** At your death, your executor and other survivors may need to learn about the debts you owed and that others owed to you during your life. For help collecting and recording this information, use Quicken WillMaker's Information for Caregivers and Survivors form.

Forgiving Debts Others Owe You

You can release anyone who owes you a debt from the responsibility of paying it back to your estate after you die. You can cancel any such debt—oral or written. If you do, your forgiveness functions much the same as giving a gift; those who were indebted to you will no longer be legally required to pay the money they owed.

Keep in mind that releasing people or institutions from the debts they owe you may diminish the property that your beneficiaries receive under your will.

Quicken WillMaker prompts you to describe any debt you wish to cancel—including the name of the person who owes it, the approximate date the debt was incurred and the amount you wish to forgive. This information is important so that the debt can be properly identified.

Explaining Your Intention

If you forgive a debt, it is likely to come as a pleasant surprise to those living with the expectation that they must repay it. And you will probably give the gesture considerable thought before including such a direction in your will. While the final document will contain a brief clause stating your intention, you may wish to explain your reasoning beyond this bald statement. If you wish to do so, it is best to write your explanation in a brief letter that you attach to your will. (See Chapter 11.)

CAUTION

Caution for married or legally partnered people. If you want to use your will to forgive a debt and the debt was incurred while you were married or legally partnered, you may only have the right to forgive half the debt. There is a special need to be cautious about this possibility in community property states. If your debt is a community property debt, you cannot cancel the whole amount due unless your spouse or partner agrees to allow you to cancel his or her share of the debt—and puts that agreement in writing.

Liabilities at Your Death

If you live owing money, chances are you will die owing money. If you do, your executor will be responsible for rounding up your property and making sure all your outstanding debts are satisfied before any of the property is put in the hands of those you have named to get it. The property you own at your death—or your estate—may be liable for several types of debts, expenses and taxes.

Debts You Owe

When you leave this credit-happy world, you will likely go out with debts you have not fully paid—personal loans, credit card bills, mortgage loans or income taxes. Whether such debts pass to the beneficiary along with the property, or must be paid out of the estate, depends upon how the debt is characterized. (See "Types of Debts," below.)

Expenses Incurred After Your Death

There are several expenses incurred after you die—including the costs of a funeral, burial or cremation and probate—which may take your survivors by surprise if you do not plan ahead for paying them.

Funeral and burial expenses, for example, typically cost several thousand dollars. And for those who do not plan ahead, the costs may soar even higher. In addition, probate and estate administration fees typically run about 5% to 7% of the value of the property you leave to others in your will.

Estate and Inheritance Taxes

Estate tax is a concern for few people. The tax is levied on the property you own at death—but a large amount of property is exempt from taxation. (See "Estate and Inheritance Taxes," below.)

Unless you specify otherwise in your will, in most states, these taxes will normally be paid proportionately out of the estate's liquid assets. This means that a beneficiary's property will be reduced by the percentage that the property bears to the total liquid assets. Liquid assets include bank accounts, money market accounts and marketable securities. Real estate and tangible personal property, such as cars, furniture and antiques are not included. This could cause a problem if, for example, you left your bank account with $50,000 in it to a favorite nephew and your tax liability—most of which resulted from valuable real property left to another beneficiary—gobbled up all or most of it.

Types of Debts

There are two basic kinds of debts to think about when making a will— secured and unsecured.

When You Need Not Worry—And When You Should

Typically, you do not need to leave instructions about debts if any of the following are true:

- Your debts and expenses are likely to be negligible—or to represent only a tiny fraction of a relatively large estate.
- You are leaving all your property to your spouse or partner or specifying that it should be shared among a very few beneficiaries, without dividing it into specific bequests.
- You understand and approve of how your state law deals with debts and expenses.

On the other hand, you may need to be concerned about covering your debts and death taxes when your will-making plan involves dividing up your property among a number of beneficiaries.

And you need to plan more carefully if debts payable by your estate are likely to be large enough to cut significantly into bequests left to individuals and charitable institutions. The danger, of course, is that unless you plan carefully, the people whose bequests are used to pay debts and expenses may be the very people whom you would have preferred to take your property free and clear.

> **EXAMPLE:** Ruth has $40,000 in a money market account and several valuable musical instruments, also worth $40,000. She makes a will leaving the money market account to her daughter and the instruments to her musician son but does not specify how her debts and expenses should be paid. Due to medical bills and an unpaid personal loan from a friend, Ruth dies owing $35,000. After Ruth's death, her executor must follow state law, which first requires that debts be paid out of the residuary estate. But because there is no residuary—all property is used up by specific bequests—a second rule applies that requires that debts be paid out of liquid assets. As a result, the executor pays the $35,000 out of the money market account, leaving the daughter with only $5,000. The son receives the $40,000 worth of musical instruments.

Secured Debts

Secured debts are any debts owed on specific property that must be paid before title to that property fully belongs to its owner.

One common type of secured debt occurs when a major asset such as a car, appliance or business is paid for over a period of time. Usually, the lender of credit will retain some measure of legal ownership in the asset—termed a security interest—until it is paid off.

Another common type of secured debt occurs when a lender, as a condition of the loan, takes a security interest in property already owned by the person applying for the money. For instance, most finance companies require their borrowers to agree to pledge "all their personal property" as security for the loan. The legal jargon for this type of security interest is a non-purchase-money secured debt—that is, the debt is incurred for a purpose other than purchasing the property that secures repayment.

Other common types of secured debts are mortgages and deeds of trust owed on real estate in exchange for a purchase or equity loan, tax liens and assessments that are owed on real estate and, in some instances, liens or legal claims on personal and real property created as a result of litigation or home repair.

If you are leaving property in your will that is subject to a secured debt, you may be concerned about whether the debt will pass to the beneficiary along with the property, or whether it must be paid by your estate.

Debts on Real Estate

Quicken WillMaker passes all secured debts owed on real estate along with the real estate.

> EXAMPLE: Paul owes $50,000 under a deed of trust on his home, signed as a condition of obtaining an equity loan. He leaves the home to his children. The deed of trust is a secured debt on real property and passes to the children along with the property.

EXAMPLE: Sonny and Cati, a married couple, borrow $100,000 from the bank to purchase their home and take out a deed of trust in the bank's favor as security for the loan. They still owe $78,000 and are two years behind in property tax payments. In separate wills, Sonny and Cati leave their ownership share to each other and name their children as alternates to take the home in equal shares. The deed of trust is a purchase money secured debt and, if the children get the property, they will also get the mortgage—and responsibility for paying the past due amount in taxes.

Debts on Personal Property

All debts owed on personal property pass to the beneficiaries of the property.

EXAMPLE: Phil owns a Ferrari. Although the car is registered in Phil's name, the bank holds legal title pending Phil's payment of the outstanding $75,000 car note. Phil uses Quicken WillMaker to leave the car to his companion Paula. The car note is a secured debt and will pass to Paula with the car.

When the Debt Exceeds the Property Value

Because the property is usually worth more than any debt secured by it, a person who takes the property at your death but does not want to owe money can sell the property, pay off the debt and pocket the difference. However, at times, relying on this approach is not satisfactory—especially when it comes to houses.

For example, if you leave your daughter your house with the hope that it will be her home, you will probably not want her to have to sell the house because she cannot meet the mortgage payments. If you think a particular beneficiary will need assistance with paying a debt owed on property, try to leave the necessary money or valuable assets to him or her as well.

Unsecured Debts

Unsecured debts are all debts not tied to specific property. Common examples are medical bills, most credit card bills, utility bills and probate fees. Your executor must pay these debts and expenses out of property from your estate. A student loan is another common example of an unsecured debt. However, most student loans can be canceled if the borrower dies before the loan is paid off, so the borrower's estate will owe nothing.

Paying Debts and Expenses

Quicken WillMaker offers two options for paying debts, including the expenses of probate. You can:

- designate a particular asset or assets to be used or sold to pay debts and expenses, or
- choose not to designate specific assets, which will mean that your executor will pay the debts and expenses as required by the laws of your state.

Designating Specific Assets

One helpful approach to taking care of debts and expenses is to designate one or more specific assets that your executor must use to pay them. For example, if you designate a savings or money market account to be used for paying off your debts and expenses, and the amount in the account is sufficient to meet these obligations, the other bequests you make in your will won't be affected by your estate's indebtedness.

If you select specific assets to pay your debts and expenses, you'll probably want to select liquid assets over nonliquid assets. Liquid assets are those easily converted into cash at full value: bank and deposit accounts, money market accounts, stocks and bonds. On the other hand, tangible assets, such as motor vehicles, planes, jewelry, stamp and coin collections, electronic items and musical instruments, must be sold to raise the necessary cash. Hurried sales seldom bring in anywhere near the full value, which means the net worth of your estate will also be reduced.

> **EXAMPLE:** Harry writes mystery books for a living. He has never produced a blockbuster but owns 15 copyrights, which produce royalties of about $70,000 a year. During his life, Harry has traveled widely and collected artifacts from around the world. They have a value of $300,000 if sold carefully to knowledgeable collectors. Harry makes a will leaving his copyrights to his spouse and the artifacts to his children. He also designates that the artifacts should be used to pay his debts and expenses—which total $150,000 at death. Harry's executor, who is not a collector and has little time or inclination to sell the artifacts one by one, sells them in bulk for $140,000—less than half of their true value. To raise the extra $10,000, two of the copyrights are sold, again at less than their true value. As a result, Harry's children receive nothing and his spouse gets less than Harry intended.

Avoid designating property you have left to specific beneficiaries. It is important to review your specific bequests before designating assets to pay debts and expenses. If possible, designate liquid assets that have not been left to specific beneficiaries. Only as a last resort should you earmark a tangible item also left in a specific bequest for first use to pay debts and expenses.

One exception to this general recommendation occurs if you believe you are unlikely to owe much when you die and that the expenses of probate will be low. Then, it makes sense for you to designate a substantial liquid asset left as a specific bequest to also pay debts and expenses.

Covering Your Debts With Insurance

One way to deal with the problem of large debts and small assets is to purchase a life insurance policy in an amount large enough to pay your anticipated debts and expenses and have the proceeds made payable to your estate. You can then specify in your will that these proceeds should be used to pay your debts and expenses—with the rest going to your residuary beneficiary or a beneficiary named in a specific bequest.

But be careful. If large sums are involved, talk with an estate planner or accountant before adopting this sort of plan. Having insurance money paid to your estate subjects that amount to probate. A better alternative may be to provide that estate assets be sold, with the proceeds used to pay the debts. Then have the insurance proceeds made payable directly to your survivors free of probate.

Of course, if the source you specify is insufficient to pay all the bills, your executor will still face the problem of which property to use to make up the difference. For this reason, it is often wise to list several resources and specify the order in which they should be used. Also, make sure that they are worth more than what is likely to be required.

EXAMPLE: Ella, a widow, makes a will that contains the following bequests:

- My house at 1111 Soto Street in Albany, New York, to Hillary Bernette. (The house has an outstanding mortgage of $50,000, for which Hillary will become responsible.)
- My coin collection (appraised at $30,000) to Stanley, Mark and Belinda Bernette.
- My three antique chandeliers to Herbert Perkins.
- The rest of my property to Denise Everread. Although not spelled out in the will, this property consists of a savings account ($26,000), a car ($5,000), a camera ($1,000) and stock ($7,000).

Using Quicken WillMaker, Ella specifies that her savings account and stock be used in the order listed to pay debts and expenses. When Ella dies, she owes $8,000; the expenses of probating her estate total $4,000. Following Ella's instructions, her executor would close the savings account, use $12,000 of it to pay debts and expenses and turn the rest over to Denise along with the stock and camera.

EXAMPLE: Now suppose Ella has only $6,000 in the savings account. When she dies, her executor, following the same instructions, would close the account ($6,000) and sell enough stock to make up the difference ($6,000). The remaining $1,000 worth of stock, the camera and the car would pass to Denise.

CAUTION

Describe property consistently. If you designate property both as a specific bequest and as a source for paying your debts, be sure to describe it exactly the same in both instances to avoid confusion.

If You Don't Specify Assets

If you do not specify how you want your debts and expenses to be paid, your executor will need to follow your state's laws, and your Quicken WillMaker will instructs him or her to do so.

Some states leave it up to your executor to make good decisions about how to pay your debts and expenses. Other states require that debts and expenses be paid first out of property in your estate that does not pass under your will. In other states, your debts and expenses must first be paid out of liquid assets, such as bank accounts and securities, then from tangible personal property and, as a last resort, from real estate.

Estate and Inheritance Taxes

Before you concentrate on how you want your estate or inheritance taxes to be paid, consider whether you need to be concerned about these types of taxes at all. Most people do not.

These taxes are imposed on the transfer of property after someone dies. Some people confuse probate-avoidance devices, such as living trusts and joint tenancy, with schemes to save on taxes. But avoiding probate does not reduce these taxes.

Whether or not your estate will be required to pay taxes depends on two factors:

- the value of your taxable estate—that is, your net estate minus any gifts or expenses that are tax-exempt, and
- the laws of the state in which you live.

Federal Estate Taxes

Only a fraction of estates end up owing federal estate tax. Primarily, that's because a large amount of property is exempt from the tax. For deaths that occur in 2009, estates smaller than $3.5 million do not owe estate tax.

Planning for estate taxes can be quite complicated. If you think your estate might be large enough to owe estate tax, see Chapter 12, which explains the system.

State Inheritance and Estate Taxes

State taxes normally do not take a deep enough bite to cause serious concern unless your estate is very large. However, because of recent changes to federal and state tax laws, an increasing number of estates owe some state tax. (Some estates may have to pay state tax even if they aren't large enough to owe federal estate tax.) If you own a lot of property—say, more than $500,000 worth—and you're concerned about it, you may want to check with an estate planning or tax lawyer who can bring you up to date on the laws in your state.

If it turns out that your estate owes state taxes, your executor has an obligation to pay them and will therefore deduct them from each bequest unless you state differently in your will, as you can do when using Quicken WillMaker.

> **SEE AN EXPERT**
>
> **Getting help with large estates.** As you might imagine, financial planning experts have devised many creative ways to plan for paying estate and inheritance taxes. If your estate is large enough to warrant concern about possible federal or state taxes, it is large enough for you to afford a consultation with an accountant, estate planning specialist or lawyer specializing in estates and trusts.

Choosing How to Pay Taxes

Quicken WillMaker offers the following options for paying estate and inheritance taxes. You can:

- pay them from all property you own at death
- designate specific assets, or
- choose not to specify how your taxes will be paid, leaving that matter up to state law.

If the value of your estate is well below the federal and state estate tax range, and you have no reasonable expectation that your estate will grow much larger before your death, you may want to skip this discussion of your options for paying taxes and choose the option "Don't specify."

If you are a relatively young, healthy person and you expect your estate to owe only a small amount of tax, you may want to adopt one of the Quicken WillMaker tax payment options now and worry about more sophisticated tax planning later. After all, by the time you die, federal and state tax rules may have changed many times.

Paying Taxes From All Property You Own

For the purpose of computing estate and inheritance tax liability, your estate consists of all property you legally own at your death, whether it passes under the terms of your will or outside of your will—such as a joint tenancy, living trust, savings bank trust or life insurance policy. Because your estate's tax liability will be computed on the basis of all this property, you may wish to have the beneficiaries of the property share proportionately in the responsibility for paying the taxes.

> **EXAMPLE:** Julie Johanssen, a widow, owns a house (worth $1 million), stocks ($400,000), jewelry ($150,000) and investments as a limited partner in a number of rental properties ($900,000). To avoid probate, Julie puts the house in a living trust for her eldest son, Warren; puts the stocks in a living trust for another son, Alain; and uses her will to leave the jewelry to a daughter, Penelope, and the investments to her two surviving brothers, Sean and Ivan. She specifies that all beneficiaries of property in her taxable estate share in paying any estate and inheritance taxes.
>
> When Julie dies, the net worth of her estate, which consists of all the property mentioned, is over the amount of the estate tax exemption in the year of her death, so there is federal estate tax liability.
>
> Each of Julie's beneficiaries will be responsible for paying a portion of this liability. Each portion will be measured by the proportion that beneficiary's inheritance has to the estate as a whole.

Designating Specific Assets

As with payment of debts and expenses, it may be a good approach to designate one or more specific property items to satisfy the amount you owe in taxes. Again, if you designate a bank, brokerage or money market account to be used for paying taxes, and the amount in the account is adequate to meet these obligations, the other bequests you make in your will should not be affected.

Of course, if the resource you specify for payment of your estate and inheritance taxes is not sufficient to cover the amount due, your executor will still face the problem of which property will be used to make up the difference. So, again, it is a good idea to list several resources that should be used to pay estate and inheritance taxes.

CAUTION
Guidance for selecting specific assets. If you do choose to select specific assets to be used to pay your taxes, follow the general rules set out in "Paying Debts and Expenses," above.

If You Don't Specify a Method of Payment

If you choose this option, your will directs your executor to pay your estate and inheritance taxes as required by the laws of your state. As with your debts and expenses, your state law controls how your executor is to approach this issue if you do not establish your own plan. Some states leave the method of payment up to your executor, while others provide that all beneficiaries must share the tax burden. Depending on your financial and tax situation and the law of your state, more variables set in than can reasonably be covered here. If you are concerned about the possible legal repercussions of choosing this option, consider researching your state's law. (See Chapter 13.)

Make It Legal: Final Steps

Once you have proceeded through all the Quicken WillMaker screens and responded to all the questions the program poses, your will is nearly finished. There are just a few more steps you must take to make it legally effective so that the directions you expressed in it can be carried out after your death.

No Accents or Umlauts

If your name contains accent marks, umlauts or other special characters, you can type them into WillMaker. *However, those characters will not show up correctly in your printed document unless you change the default font* (Times New Roman). Common Windows fonts that will correctly print special characters include:

- Georgia (serif), and
- Verdana (sans serif).

For details on how to change the fonts of printed documents, see "Changing How Your Documents Look" in Part 7 of the Users' Manual.

Checking Your Will

Before you sign your will, take some time to scrutinize it and make sure it accurately expresses your wishes. You can do this either by previewing it in the program or by printing out a draft copy. (Consult the Users' Manual if you need additional guidance.)

> ### Having an Expert Check Your Will
>
> You may want to have your will checked by an attorney or tax expert. This makes good sense if you are left with nagging questions about the legal implications of your choices, or if you own a great deal of property or have a complicated idea of how you want to leave it. But keep in mind that you are your own best expert on most issues and decisions involved in making a will—what property you own, your relation to family members and friends and your own favorite charities. Also, some attorneys don't support the self-help approach to making a will, so you may have to find one who is cooperative. (See Chapter 13.)

Signing and Witnessing Requirements

To be valid, a will must be legally executed. This means that you must sign your will in front of two witnesses. These witnesses must sign the will not only in your presence, but also in the presence of all the other witnesses.

Requirements for Witnesses

There are a few legal requirements for witnesses. The witnesses need to be of sound mind. In most states, the witnesses need to be 18 or older. Many states also require that the witnesses not be people who will take property under the will. Thus, we require that you not use as a witness someone to whom you leave property in your will, even as an alternate or residuary beneficiary.

As a matter of common sense, the people you choose to be witnesses should be easily available when you die. While this bit of future history is impossible to foretell with certainty, it is usually best to choose witnesses who are in good health, are younger than you are and likely to remain in your geographic area. However, the witnesses do not have to be residents of your state.

The Self-Proving Option

For a will to be accepted by a probate court, the executor must show that the document really is the will of the person it purports to be—a process called proving the will. In the past, all wills were proved either by having one or two witnesses come into court to testify or swear in written, notarized statements called affidavits that they saw you sign your will.

Today, most states allow people to make their wills self-proving—that is, they can be admitted in probate court without the hassle of herding up witnesses to appear in court or sign affidavits. This is accomplished when the person making the will and the witnesses all appear before a notary public and sign an affidavit under oath, verifying that all necessary formalities for execution have been satisfied.

If you live in a state that offers the self-proving option, Quicken WillMaker automatically produces the correct affidavit for your state, with accompanying instructions. With the exception of New Hampshire, the self-proving affidavit is not part of your will, but a separate document. To use it, you and your witnesses must first sign the will as discussed above. Then, you and your witnesses must sign the self-proving affidavit in front of a notary public. This may be done any time after the will is signed but, obviously, it is easiest to do it while all your witnesses are gathered together to watch you sign your will. Most notaries will charge at least a minimal amount for their services—and will require you and your witnesses to present some identification verifying that you are who you claim to be.

Many younger people—who are likely to make a number of wills before they die—decide not to make their wills self-proving, due to the initial trouble of getting a notary at the signing. If you are one of these people, file the uncompleted affidavit and instructions in a safe place in case you change your mind later.

Note for California and Indiana Readers

In California or Indiana, the self-proving feature does not require a separate affidavit. Instead, the fact that the witnesses sign the will under the oath printed above their signatures is sufficient to have the will admitted into probate, unless a challenge is mounted. There is no need to take further steps to make a California or Indiana will self-proving.

States Without Self-Proving Laws

The self-proving option is not available in the District of Columbia, Maryland, Ohio or Vermont. In these states, your executor will be required to prove your will.

Signing Procedure

You need not utter any magic words when signing your will and having it witnessed, but a few legal requirements suggest the best way to proceed:

- Gather all witnesses together in one place.
- Inform your witnesses that the papers you hold in your hand are your last will and testament. This is important, because the laws in many states specifically require that you acknowledge the document as your will before the witnesses sign it. The witnesses need not read your will, however, and there is no need for them to know its contents. If you want to ensure that the contents of the will stay confidential, you may cover all but the signature portion of your will with a separate sheet of paper while the witnesses sign.
- Initial each page of the will at the bottom on the lines provided. The purpose of initialing is to prevent anyone from challenging

the will as invalid on the grounds that changes were made to it by someone else.

- Sign the last page on the signature line while the witnesses watch. Use the same form of your name that you stated in your will.
- Ask each of the witnesses to initial the bottom of each page on a line there, then watch as they sign and fill in their addresses on the last page where indicated. Their initials act as evidence if anyone later claims you changed your will without going through the proper legal formalities.

Changing Your Quicken WillMaker Will

Once you have signed your will and had it witnessed, it is extremely important that you do not alter it by inserting handwritten or typed additions or changes. Do not even correct misspellings. The laws of most states require that after a will is signed, any additions or changes to it, even clerical ones, must be made by following the same signing and witnessing requirements as for an original will.

Although it is legally possible to make handwritten corrections on your will before you sign it, that is a bad idea since, after your death, it will not be clear to the probate court that you made the corrections before the will was signed. The possibility that the changes were made later may throw the legality of the whole will into question.

If you want to make changes after your will has been signed and witnessed, there are two ways to accomplish it: You can either make a new will or make a formal addition, called a codicil, to the existing one. Either approach requires a new round of signing and witnessing.

One of the great advantages of Quicken WillMaker is that you can conveniently keep current by simply making a new will. This does away with the need to tack on changes to the will in the form of a codicil and involves no need for additional gyrations. Codicils are not a good idea when using Quicken WillMaker because of the possibility of creating a conflict between the codicil and the original will. It is simpler and safer to make a revised Quicken WillMaker will, sign it and have it witnessed. (See "How to Make a New Will" in Chapter 10.)

Storing Your Will

Once your will is properly signed and witnessed, be sure that your executor can easily locate it at your death. Here are some suggestions:

- Store your printed and witnessed will in an envelope on which you have typed your name and the word "Will."
- Place the envelope in a fireproof metal box, file cabinet or home safe. An alternative is to place the original will in a safe deposit box. But before doing that, learn the bank's policy about access to the box after your death. If, for instance, the safe deposit box is in your name alone, the box can probably be opened only by a person authorized by a court, and then only in the presence of a bank employee. An inventory may even be required if any person enters the box or for state tax purposes. All of this takes time, and in the meantime, your document will be locked away from those who need it.

Helping Others Find Your Will

Your will should be easy to locate at your death. You want to spare your survivors the anxiety of having to search for your will when they are already dealing with the grief of losing you. Make sure your executor and at least one other person you trust know where to find your will.

Making Copies of Your Will

Some people are tempted to prepare more than one signed and witnessed original of their wills in case one is lost. While it is legal in most states to prepare and sign duplicate originals, it is never a good idea. Common sense tells you why: If you later want to change your will, it can be difficult to locate all the old copies to destroy them.

That said, it is sometimes a good idea to make several unsigned copies of your current will. You may want to give one to your executor or other loved ones, so they know your plans.

To share your will, print multiple copies when you finalize your document. Print these copies with a "duplicate" watermark; see Part 4 of the Users' Manual for instructions. Sign your original will and distribute the unsigned copies. We also recommend that you store one unsigned copy with your original will.

If you need more copies later, you can photocopy the unsigned will or print copies from your computer by returning to the program.

Of course, you aren't required to disclose the contents of your will to anyone. If you prefer to keep your will confidential until your death, do not make any copies.

Updating Your Will

Your will is an extremely personal document. Information such as your marital status, where you live, the property you own and whether you have children—all are examples of life choices that affect what you include in your will and what laws will be applied to enforce it.

Life wreaks havoc on even the best-laid plans. You may sell one house and buy another. You may divorce. You may have or adopt children. Eventually you will face the grief of losing a loved one. Not all life changes require you to change your will. However, significant ones often do. This chapter tells you when it's necessary to make a new will.

When to Make a New Will

The following occurrences signal that it is time for you to make a new will.

Marrying or Divorcing

Suppose that after you use Quicken WillMaker to leave all or part of your property to your spouse, you get divorced. Under the law in many states, the divorce automatically cancels the bequest to the former spouse. The alternate beneficiary named for that bequest or, if there is none your residuary beneficiary, gets the property. In some states, however, your former spouse would still be entitled to take your property as directed in the will. If you remarry, state legal rules become even more murky. (In a few states, these rules also apply to registered domestic partners.)

Rather than deal with all these complexities, follow this simple rule: Make a new will if you marry, divorce, are separated and seriously considering divorce or if you register or dissolve a domestic partnership.

SEE AN EXPERT

Beware of state laws on spouses' shares. If you leave your spouse or registered domestic partner out of your will because you are separated, and you die before you become divorced, it is possible that the spouse or partner could claim a statutory share of your estate. (See "Your Spouse's Right to Inherit From You" in Chapter 4.) Consult a lawyer to find out how the laws of your state apply to this situation. (See Chapter 13.)

Getting or Losing Property

If you leave all your property in a lump to one or more people or organizations, there is no need to change your will if you acquire new items of property or get rid of existing ones. Those individuals or organizations take all of your property at your death, without regard to what it is.

But if you have made specific bequests of property that you no longer own, it is wise to make a new will. If you leave a specific item—a particular Tiffany lamp, for example—to someone, but you no longer own the item when you die, the person named in your will to receive it may be out of luck. In most states, that person is not entitled to receive another item or money instead. In some states, however, the law presumes that you wanted the beneficiary to have something—and so gives him or her the right to a sum of money equal to the value of the gift. While this may be what you want, it could still disrupt your plan for how you want your property distributed. The legal word for a bequest that fails to make it in this way is ademption. People who do not get to take the property in question are often heard to use an earthier term.

However, in some circumstances, if a specific item has merely changed form, the original beneficiary may still have a claim to it. Examples of this are:

- a promissory note that has been paid and for which the cash is still available, and
- a house that is sold in exchange for a promissory note and deed of trust.

A problem similar to ademption occurs when there is not enough money to go around. For example, if you leave $50,000 each to your spouse and two children, but there is only $90,000 in your estate at your death, the gifts in the will must all be reduced. In legal lingo, this is called an abatement. How property is abated under state law is often problematic.

You can avoid these problems if you adjust the type and amount of your bequests to reflect reality—a task that may require both diligence and the commitment to make a new will periodically.

Adding or Losing Children

Each time a child is born or legally adopted into your family, the new child should be named in the will—where you are asked to name your children—and provided for according to your wishes. If you do not do this, the child might later challenge your will in court, claiming that he or she was overlooked as an heir and is entitled to a substantial share of your property. (See "Your Children" in Chapter 3.)

If any of your children die before you and leave children, you should name those grandchildren in your will. If they are not mentioned in your will, they might later be legally entitled to claim a share of your estate. (See "Your Grandchildren" in Chapter 3.)

Moving to a Different State

Quicken WillMaker applies several state-specific laws when it helps you create your will. These laws are especially important in two situations.

- If you have set up one form of management for young beneficiaries and then move to a different state, you may find when making a new will that Quicken WillMaker presents you with different management options. This is because some states have adopted the Uniform Transfers to Minors Act and others have not. If you want to see whether your new state offers different management options, see "The Uniform Transfers to Minors Act" in Chapter 6.
- If you are married and do not intend to leave all or most of your property to your spouse, review "Property Rules for Married People" in Chapter 4, which discusses the rules if you move from a community property state to a common law state or vice versa.

Losing Beneficiaries

If a beneficiary you have named to receive a significant amount of property dies before you, you should make a new will. It is especially important to do this if you named only one beneficiary for a bequest and did not name an alternate—or if the alternate you named is no longer your first choice to get the property.

Losing Guardians or Property Managers

The first choice or alternate named to serve as a personal guardian for your minor children or those you have named to manage their property may move away, become disabled or simply turn out to be unsuitable for the job. If so, you will probably want to make a new will naming a different person.

Losing an Executor

The executor of your estate is responsible for making sure your will provisions are carried out. If you decide that the executor you originally named is no longer suitable—or if he or she dies before you do—you should make a new will in which you name another person for the job.

Losing Witnesses

The witnesses who sign your will are responsible for testifying that the signature on your will is valid and that you appeared capable of making a will when you did so. If two or more of your witnesses become unable to fulfill this function, you may want to make a new will with new witnesses—especially if you have some inkling that anyone is likely to contest your will after you die. But a new will is probably not necessary if you have made your will self-proving. (See "The Self-Proving Option" in Chapter 9.)

How to Make a New Will

It is easy to make a new will using Quicken WillMaker. In fact, a subsequent swoop through the program will proceed even more quickly than the first time through, since you will know what to expect and will likely be familiar with many of the legal concepts you had to learn at first.

If you review your will and wish to change some of your answers, the program will automatically alert you to specific changes that may signal different laws applying to your situation. These include changes in:

- your marital or domestic partner status
- your state of residence
- the number of children you have, and
- your general approach to will making—from simple to complex, or vice versa.

If you make a new will, even if it only involves a few changes, you must follow the legal requirements for having it signed and witnessed just as if you were starting from scratch. If you choose to make your will self-proving, you must also complete a new affidavit.

CAUTION

In with the new, out with the old. As soon as you print, sign and have your new will witnessed, it will legally replace all wills you have made before it. But to avoid possible confusion, you should physically destroy all other original wills and any copies of them.

Explanatory Letters

I n addition to the tasks that you can accomplish in a Quicken WillMaker will, you may also wish to:

- explain why you are giving property to certain beneficiaries and not to others
- explain disparities in bequests
- express positive or negative sentiments about a beneficiary
- express wishes about how to care for a pet
- explain how shared gifts should be divided, or
- leave your loved ones a statement about your personal experiences, values or beliefs.

Quicken WillMaker does not allow you to do these things in your will for one important reason: The program has been written, tested and tested again with painstaking attention to helping you make your own legal and unambiguous will. If you add general information, personal statements or reasons for making or not making a bequest, you risk the possibility of producing a document with conflicting, confusing or possibly even illegal provisions.

Fortunately, there is a way you can have a final say about personal matters without seriously risking your will's legal integrity. You can write a letter to accompany your will expressing your thoughts to those who survive you.

Since what you put in the letter will not have legal effect as part of your will, there is little danger that your expressions will tread upon the time-tested legal language of the will or cause other problems later. In fact, if your will is ambiguous and your statement in the letter sheds some light on your intentions, judges may use the letter to help clarify your will. However, if your statements in the letter fully contradict provisions in your will, you may create interpretation problems after your death. For example, if you cut your daughter out of your will and also state in a letter attached to the will that she is your favorite child and that is why you are leaving her the family home, you are setting the stage for future confusion.

Keeping these cautions in mind, writing a letter to those who survive you to explain why you wrote your will as you did—and knowing they will read your reasoning at your death—can give you a great deal of peace of mind during life. It may also help explain potential slights and hurt feelings of surviving friends and family members. This chapter offers some guidance on how you can write a clear letter that expresses your wishes without jeopardizing the legality of your will.

An Introduction for Your Letter

A formal introduction to the letter you leave can help make it clear that what you write is an expression of your sentiments and not intended as a will—or an addition to or interpretation of your will.

After the introduction, you are free to express your sentiments, keeping in mind that your estate may be held liable for any false, derogatory statements you make about an individual or organization.

One suggested introduction follows.

To My Executor:

This letter expresses my feelings and reasons for certain decisions made in my will. It is not my will, nor do I intend it to be an interpretation of my will. My will, which I signed, dated and had witnessed on _____ , is the sole expression of my intentions concerning all my property and other matters covered in it.

Should anything I say in this letter conflict with, or seem to conflict with, any provision of my will, the will shall be followed.

I request that you give a copy of this letter to each person named in my will to take property, or act as a guardian or custodian, and to anyone else you determine should receive a copy.

Expressing Sentiments and Explaining Choices

There is little that a manual such as this can say to guide you in personal expressions of the heart. What follows are some suggestions about topics you might wish to cover.

Explaining Why Gifts Were Made

The Quicken WillMaker requirement that you must keep descriptions of property and beneficiaries short and succinct may leave you unsatisfied. You may have thought hard and long about why you want a particular person to get particular property—and feel frustrated that you are constrained in your will to listing your wishes in a few simple words. You can remedy that by explaining your feelings in a letter.

EXAMPLE:

[Introduction]

The gift of my fishing boat to my friend Hank is in remembrance of the many companionable days we enjoyed fishing together on the lake. Hank, I hope you're out there for many more years.

EXAMPLE:

[Introduction]

Julie, the reason I have given you the farm is that you love it as much as I do and I know you'll do your best to make sure it stays in the family. But please, if the time comes when personal or family concerns mean that it makes sense to sell it, do so with a light heart—and knowing that it's just what I would have done.

Explaining Disparities in Gifts

You may also wish to explain your reasons for leaving more property to one person than another. While it is certainly your prerogative to make or not make bequests as you wish, you can also guess that in a number of family situations, unbalanced shares may cause hurt feelings or hostility after your death.

Ideally, you could call those involved together during your life, explaining to them why you plan to leave your property as you do. However, if you wish to keep your property plans private until after you die—or would find such a meeting too painful or otherwise impossible—you can attach a letter of explanation to your will.

EXAMPLE:

> [Introduction]
>
> I love all my children equally. The reason I gave a smaller ownership share in the house to Tim than to my other children is that Tim received family funds to purchase his own home, so it is fair that my other two children receive more of my property now.

EXAMPLE:

> [Introduction]
>
> I am giving the bulk of my property to my son Jason for one reason: Because of his health problems, he needs it more.
>
> Ted and Ellen, I love you just as much, and I am extremely proud of the life choices you have made. But the truth is that you two can manage fine without a boost from me, and Jason cannot.

Offering Suggestions for Shared Gifts

If you are leaving a shared gift that contains a number of specific items—such as "my household furnishings" or "my art collection"—you may have some thoughts on how you'd like your beneficiaries to divide up the property. Of course, you can use your will to control the size of the share that each beneficiary gets, but that that still leaves your survivors to figure out who gets which specific assets. For example, if you leave your entire estate to be shared equally by your three children, how should your executor decide who gets the house, who gets the bank accounts and who gets the cars?

You can use a letter to make suggestions to your executor about how you want your property divided. Your suggestions will not have any legal weight; your executor is required to follow the terms of your will, not the terms of your letter. However, your letter can give your executor valuable guidance about how to distribute property, within the terms of your will.

Even if you don't particularly care who gets which things, you may want to suggest a fair way of figuring it out, such as a lottery for the highly coveted items.

Whatever suggestions you give, be very careful not to contradict any of the gifts you make in your will.

EXAMPLE:

[Introduction]

I have left my library equally to my grandchildren. I know each of them has enjoyed many of the books over the years and I want to make sure that each receives a few favorites. I suggest that you hold a drawing to determine the order in which each grandchild will choose a book, with each then taking a volume in turn until their favorites are spoken for. The rest of the library can be distributed—taken or given away—in whatever manner they choose.

Expressing Positive or Negative Sentiments

Whatever your plans for leaving your property, you may wish to attach a letter to your will in which you clear your mind of some sentiments you formed during life. These may be positive —thanking a loved one for kind acts. Or they may be negative—explaining why you are leaving a person out of your will.

EXAMPLE:

> [Introduction]
>
> The reason I left $10,000 to my physician Dr. Buski is not only that she treated me competently over the years, but that she was unfailingly gentle and attentive. I always appreciated that she made herself available—day or night—and took the time to explain my ailments and treatments to me.

EXAMPLE:

> [Introduction]
>
> I am leaving nothing to my brother Malcolm. I wish him no ill will. But over the years, he has decided to isolate himself from me and the rest of the family and I don't feel I owe him anything.

Supporting Your Same-Sex Marriage

If you and your partner got married and then moved to a state that doesn't recognize your marriage, you may want to attach a signed letter to your will that expresses your wish that your partner be treated in all ways as your legal spouse. This letter won't change how your property is distributed by your will, but it will make your intention clear. The note is simply a way to avoid confusion by stating that you were legally married and you consider your partner to be your spouse. It can be as brief as the sample below, or you can write more if you'd like to express your feelings about your relationship or its legal status.

EXAMPLE:

[Introduction]

Jennifer Jones and I were legally married on March 12, 2007, in the state of Massachusetts. In 2009, we moved to Kansas, which does not currently recognize our marriage. No matter where we live, I consider Jennifer my legal spouse, and it is my wish that she be treated for all purposes, including inheritance, as my legal spouse.

Explaining Choices About Your Pet

As discussed in Chapter 3, the best way to provide a home for your pet is to use your will to name a caretaker for your pet and leave some money to that person to cover the costs of your pet's care. If you like, you can use your explanatory letter to say why you chose a particular person to watch over your animals after your death.

EXAMPLE:

[Introduction]

I have left my dog Cessna to my neighbor Belinda Mason because she has been a loving friend to him, taking care of him when I was on vacation or unwell. I know that Belinda and her three children will provide a caring and happy home for Cessna when I no longer can.

Leaving Details About Your Pet's Care

You may want to provide your pet's caretaker with information and suggestions about your pet's habits and needs. We recommend that you use Quicken WillMaker's Information for Survivors and Caregivers form for this purpose. It allows you to leave specifics about each animal, including health needs, food and exercise requirements and sleeping habits. You can also use the document to describe memorial plans or final arrangements for your pet.

Describing Personal Experiences and Values

Many people are interested in leaving behind more than just property. If you wish, you can also leave a statement about the experiences, values and beliefs that have shaped your life. This kind of letter or document is often known as an "ethical will," and it can be of great worth to those who survive you.

While you could legally include an ethical will statement in your regular will—that is, the one you make to leave your property to others—we recommend that you include these sentiments in your explanatory letter or in a separate document. The reasons are the same as those mentioned earlier: It's better to avoid including anything potentially confusing or ambiguous in your legal will.

As long as you don't contradict the provisions of your legal will, your options for expressing yourself are limited only by the time and energy you have for the project. You could do something as simple as use your explanatory letter to set out a concise description of your basic values. Or, if you feel inspired, you may leave something much more detailed for your loved ones. Many survivors are touched to learn about important life stories, memories and events. You might also consider including photographs or other mementos with your letter. If writing things down seems like too much effort, you could use an audio or videotape to talk to those who are closest to you. A little thought will surely yield many creative ways to express yourself to those you care for.

RESOURCE

More information about ethical wills. If you want to go beyond writing down some of your experiences and values in your explanatory letter, there is a growing body of websites and literature that can help you explore different ways of making an ethical will. You might begin by visiting www. ethicalwill.com. The site offers some basic free information and sells kits for writing ethical wills.

When You May Need More Than a Will

P reparing a basic will, like the one you make with this program, is the essential first step in planning any estate. You may want to do more, however—especially if you own a large amount of property. In particular, when you make your will, you may want to take another look at your situation and possibly do some additional estate planning to:

- avoid probate
- reduce estate taxes, and
- control how property left to one or more beneficiaries can be used.

If you have little to leave your survivors you probably don't need to do any planning beyond making a basic will, powers of attorney and health care directives. (See "Other Must-Have Documents" in Chapter 1.) But, if your estate is moderate to large, you should think about planning to avoid probate. Putting to work even a few simple probate avoidance devices can save your inheritors a bundle.

The next step—tax planning—is more complicated, but it's something you won't need to worry about unless you own substantial property. For deaths in 2009, only estates worth more than $3.5 million dollars will owe federal estate tax. As of the writing of this manual, the future of the federal estate tax is uncertain, but exemption amounts are likely to remain high in coming years.

If you have reason to want to place controls on the property you leave, you'll most likely want to see a good estate planning lawyer.

Avoiding Probate

You may have heard or read that you ought to avoid probate—and that if you don't take steps to do so, your survivors will surely waste a lot of time and money after your death. This section will help you understand what probate is and why you may want to steer your estate away from it.

What Is Probate?

Probate is the legal process that includes filing a deceased person's will with a court, locating and gathering assets, paying debts and taxes and eventually distributing what's left as the will directs. Unless the estate qualifies as "small" under the terms of a state's law, all property left by will must go through probate. If there is no will and no probate avoidance devices are used, property is distributed according to state law—and it still must go through probate.

Fortunately, there are many devices you can use to keep property out of probate, including revocable living trusts, joint tenancy, pay-on-death beneficiary designations, and others. Property transferred by any of these methods can be given directly to the people slated to get it at your death—no court proceedings required.

Why Avoid Probate?

Probate has many drawbacks and few advantages. It's usually costly, involving fees for attorneys, appraisers, accountants and the probate court. The cost of probate varies widely from state to state, but fees can eat up about 5% of your estate, leaving that much less to go to the people you want to get it. If the estate is complicated, the fees can be even larger.

The Cost of Probate	
If you leave property worth:	**Probate may cost about:**
$200,000	$10,000
$500,000	$25,000

At least as bad as the expense of probate is the delay it causes. In many states, probate can take a year or two, during which time beneficiaries generally get nothing unless the judge allows the immediate family a small "family allowance."

If you own real estate in more than one state, it's usually necessary to have a whole separate probate proceeding in each state. That means the surviving relatives must probably find and hire a lawyer in each state and pay for multiple probate proceedings.

From the family's point of view, probate's headaches are rarely justified. If the estate contains common kinds of property—a house, stocks, bank accounts, a small business, cars—and no relatives or creditors are fighting about it, the property merely needs to be handed over to the new owners. In the vast majority of cases, the probate process entails nothing more than tedious paperwork, and the attorney is nothing more than a very highly paid clerk.

Basic Living Trusts: A Popular Way to Avoid Probate

If you've heard something about living trusts but wonder exactly what they are and how they work, this section will give you a quick lesson.

First of all, what's a trust? It's an arrangement under which one person, called the trustee, owns property on behalf of someone else, called the beneficiary. You can create a trust simply by preparing and signing a document called a Declaration of Trust.

What, then, is a living trust? It's a trust that you set up during your lifetime to avoid probate. Living trusts sometimes go by a Latin name—"inter vivos" (among the living)—because they're created while you're alive, not at your death like some other kinds of trusts. They're also sometimes called "revocable living trusts" because you can revoke them at any time.

You can make an individual living trust or a trust that is shared with your spouse or partner.

How a Basic Living Trust Works

A basic revocable trust does, essentially, what a will does: leaves your property to the people you want to inherit it. But because a trustee owns your property, your assets don't have to go through probate at your death.

More Advantages of Living Trusts

In addition to avoiding probate, a living trust offers other benefits.

Avoiding the need for a conservator or guardianship. A living trust can be useful if you become incapacitated and unable to manage your own financial affairs. That's because the person you name as trustee (or the other grantor, if you make a shared trust) can take over management of trust assets, watching over the property for your benefit.

If there is no living trust and you haven't made other arrangements for someone to take over your finances if you become incapacitated, such as preparing a durable power of attorney for finances, a court will have to appoint someone to do the job. Typically, the spouse or adult child of the person seeks this authority and is called a conservator or guardian.

Keeping your estate plan confidential. When your will is filed with the probate court after you die, it becomes a matter of public record. A living trust, on the other hand, is a private document in most states. Because the living trust document is never filed with a court or other government entity, what you leave to whom remains private. (There is one exception: Records of real estate transfers are always public.)

Some states require you to register your living trust with the local court, but there are no penalties if you don't. The only way your trust might become public is if—and this is very unlikely—someone files a lawsuit to challenge the trust or collect a court judgment you owe.

When you create a revocable living trust, you appoint yourself trustee, with full power to manage trust property. Then you transfer ownership of some or all of your property to yourself as trustee. You keep absolute control over the property held in trust. You can:

- sell, mortgage or give away property held in trust
- put ownership of trust property back in your name
- add property to the trust
- change the beneficiaries
- name a different successor trustee, or
- revoke the trust completely.

If you and your spouse or partner create a trust together, both of you must consent to changes, although either of you is permitted to revoke the entire trust.

After you die, the person you named in your trust document to be "successor trustee" takes over. This person transfers the trust property to the relatives, friends or charities you named as the trust beneficiaries. No probate is necessary for property that was held in trust. In most cases, the whole thing can be handled within a few weeks. When the property has all been transferred to the beneficiaries, the living trust ceases to exist.

If any of your beneficiaries inherit trust property while still young, the successor trustee (or the surviving grantor of a shared trust) will probably have more responsibility, following instructions you leave in the trust to manage the property until the beneficiaries are old enough to inherit it outright.

Do You Really Need a Living Trust?

Here are some factors to think about when deciding whether a living trust is right for you:

Your age. If you're under 60 and healthy, it often makes sense to prepare a will, use simple probate-avoidance devices such as joint tenancy and pay-on-death bank accounts for some property and leave the more complicated estate planning until later.

The size of your estate. The bigger your estate, the bigger the potential probate cost and the less likely that your estate will qualify for simplified probate proceedings, discussed below. Often it makes good sense to concentrate effort on making sure that major assets, such as real estate or business assets, are owned in a way that will avoid probate.

The type of property you own. You don't need a trust to avoid probate for assets like your bank and retirement accounts, and many other types of property. Take some time to learn a little bit about other types of probate avoidance devices before you jump into preparing a living trust; see "Other Ways to Avoid Probate," below.

Why You Still Need a Will

A living trust cannot completely replace a will. Even if you want to use a living trust to pass all of your property, there are reasons why you need a will, too.

Naming a guardian for minor children. You can't nominate a personal guardian for your young children in a living trust; you need a will in which to do this. (See "Personal Guardians for Your Minor Children" in Chapter 3.)

Passing property not included in the trust. A living trust works to pass only property you transfer to the trust's name. Property you may receive in the future, but do not have title to now, cannot be transferred unless you add it to the living trust later. For example, if you have inherited property from a relative that is still tied up in probate, or you expect to receive money from the settlement of a lawsuit, you need a will in case something happens to you tomorrow. And because you cannot accurately predict what property you might receive shortly before death, it's smart to back up a living trust with a will.

RESOURCE

How to make your own living trust. Nolo offers several tools that allow you to make your own individual or shared basic living trust:

Nolo's Online Living Trust, available at www.nolo.com. We'll walk you step-by-step through the process of making a living trust online. You can print your trust and all the instructions you need to finalize it and make it legal.

Living Trust Maker. If you'd rather make your trust with downloadable software, this is the option for you. You can find Living Trust Maker on Nolo's website at www.nolo.com.

Make Your Own Living Trust, by Denis Clifford. This bestselling book with CD-ROM shows you how to make the right living trust for your situation. Find it at www.nolo.com or through your favorite bookseller.

Other Ways to Avoid Probate

Here are some methods you might want to investigate, to use with or instead of a living trust.

Pay-on-Death Bank Accounts

Payable-on-death bank accounts offer one of the easiest ways to keep money—even large sums of it—out of probate. All you need to do is fill out a simple form, provided by the bank, naming the person you want to inherit the money in the account at your death.

As long as you are alive, the person you named to inherit the money in a payable-on-death (P.O.D.) account has no rights to it. You can spend the money, name a different beneficiary or close the account. At your death, the beneficiary just goes to the bank, shows proof of the death and of his or her identity and collects whatever funds are in the account. The probate court is never involved.

Transfer-on-Death Registration of Securities

Every state but Texas has adopted a law (the Uniform Transfer-on-Death Securities Registration Act) that lets you name someone to inherit your stocks, bonds or brokerage accounts without probate. It works very much like a payable-on-death bank account. When you register your ownership, either with the stockbroker or the company itself, you make a request to take ownership in what's called "beneficiary form." When the papers that show your ownership are issued, they will also show the name of your beneficiary.

After you register ownership this way, the beneficiary has no rights to the stock as long as you are alive. You are free to sell it, give it away or name a different beneficiary. But on your death, the beneficiary can claim the securities without probate, simply by providing proof of death and some identification to the broker or transfer agent. (A transfer agent is a business that is authorized by a corporation to handle stock transfers.)

Transfer-on-Death Deeds for Real Estate

In Arizona, Arkansas, Colorado, Kansas, Minnesota, Missouri, Montana, Nevada, New Mexico, Ohio, Oklahoma and Wisconsin, you can prepare a deed now but have it take effect only at your death. These transfer-on-death deeds must be prepared, signed, notarized and recorded (filed in the county land records office) just like a regular deed. But unlike a regular deed, you can revoke a transfer-on-death deed. The deed must expressly state that it does not take effect until death.

Check your state's statute for the rules. Several of the statutes provide deed forms.

Transfer-on-Death Registration for Vehicles

So far, only California, Connecticut, Indiana (watercraft only), Kansas, Missouri, Nevada and Ohio offer vehicle owners the sensible option of naming a beneficiary, right on the certificate of title or title application, to inherit a vehicle. If you do this, the beneficiary you name has no rights as long as you are alive. You are free to sell or give away a car, or name someone else as the beneficiary.

To name a transfer-on-death beneficiary, all you do is apply for registration in "beneficiary form." The new certificate lists the name of the beneficiary, who will automatically own the vehicle after your death. You can find more information on the website of your state's motor vehicles department.

Retirement Plans

Retirement plans such as IRAs, 401(k)s and Keoghs, don't have to go through probate. All you need to do is name a beneficiary to receive the funds at your death, and no probate will be necessary.

Life Insurance

Life insurance proceeds are subject to probate only if the beneficiary named in the policy is your estate. That's done occasionally if the estate will need immediate cash to pay debts and taxes, but it's usually counterproductive.

Joint Tenancy

Joint tenancy is an efficient and practical way to transfer some kinds of property without probate.

Joint tenancy is a way two or more people can hold title to property they own together. All joint owners (called joint tenants) must own equal shares of the property. (Vermont and Connecticut are exceptions; joint owners there may own unequal shares.) When one joint owner dies, the surviving owners automatically get complete ownership of the property. This is called the "right of survivorship." The property doesn't go through probate court—there is only some simple paperwork to fill out to transfer the property into the name of the surviving owner.

A will doesn't affect who inherits joint tenancy property. So even if your will leaves your half-interest in joint tenancy property to someone else, the surviving owners will still inherit it.

This rule isn't as ironclad as it may sound. You can, while still alive, break the joint tenancy by transferring your interest in the property to someone else (or, in some states, to yourself, but not as a joint tenant).

Joint tenancy often works well when couples acquire real estate or other valuable property together. If they take title in joint tenancy, probate is avoided when the first owner dies—though not (unlike a living trust) when the second owner dies.

Joint tenancy is usually a poor estate planning device when an older person, seeking only to avoid probate, puts solely owned property into joint tenancy with someone else. If you make someone else a co-owner, in joint tenancy, of property that you now own yourself, you give up half ownership of the property. The new owner has rights that you can't take back. For example, the new owner can sell or mortgage his or her share. And federal gift tax may be assessed on the transfer.

There can also be serious problems if one joint tenant becomes incapacitated and cannot make decisions. The other owners must get legal authority to sell or mortgage the property. That may mean going to court to get someone (called a conservator or guardian, in most states) appointed to manage the incapacitated person's affairs. (This problem can be partially dealt with if the joint tenant has signed a document called a "durable power of attorney," giving someone authority to manage such affairs if he or she cannot.) With a living trust, if you (the grantor) become incapacitated, the successor trustee (or the other spouse, if you made a trust together) takes over and has full authority to manage the property. No court proceedings are necessary.

Several states have abolished or restricted joint tenancy; see below.

State Restrictions on Joint Tenancy	
Alaska	No joint tenancies for real estate, except for husband and wife, who may own property as tenants by the entirety. (See below.)
Oregon	A transfer of real estate to husband and wife creates a tenancy by the entirety, not joint tenancy. All other transfers in joint tenancy create a tenancy in common. (See "Property You Own With Others," in Chapter 4.)
Tennessee	A transfer of real estate to husband and wife creates a tenancy by the entirety, not joint tenancy. All other transfers in joint tenancy create a tenancy in common. (See "Property You Own With Others," in Chapter 4.)
Texas	A joint tenancy can be created only if you sign a separate written agreement.
Wisconsin	No joint tenancies between spouses after January 1, 1986. If spouses attempt to create a joint tenancy, it will be treated as community property with right of survivorship. (See below.)

Tenancy by the Entirety

"Tenancy by the entirety" is a form of property ownership that is similar to joint tenancy. About half the states offer it, and it is limited to married couples or same-sex couples who have registered with the state (in states that allow this).

States That Allow Tenancy by the Entirety

Alaska[1]	Maryland	Oklahoma
Arkansas	Massachusetts	Oregon[1]
Delaware[1]	Michigan	Pennsylvania
Dist. of Col.	Mississippi	Rhode Island
Florida	Missouri	Tennessee
Hawaii	New Jersey	Utah[1]
Illinois[1]	New York[1]	Vermont
Indiana[1]	North Carolina	Virginia
Kentucky[1]	Ohio[2]	Wyoming

[1] Allowed for real estate only.

[2] Only if created before April 4, 1985.

Tenancy by the entirety has many of the same advantages and disadvantages of joint tenancy and is most useful in the same kind of situation: when a couple acquires property together. When one owner dies, the surviving co-owner inherits the property. The property doesn't go through probate.

If property is held in tenancy by the entirety, neither spouse or partner can transfer his or her half of the property alone, either while alive or by will or trust. It must go to the survivor. (This is different from joint tenancy; a joint tenant is free to transfer his or her share to someone else during his or her life.)

> EXAMPLE: Fred and Ethel hold title to their house in tenancy by the entirety. If Fred wanted to sell or give away his half-interest in the house, he could not do so without Ethel's signature on the deed.

Community Property With Right of Survivorship

In a few states, married couples (and in California, registered domestic partners) can own property together "as community property with right of survivorship." When one spouse dies, the other automatically inherits the property, without probate. The states that offer this option are Alaska, Arizona, California, Nevada and Wisconsin.

Simplified Probate Proceedings

Many states have begun, slowly, to dismantle some of the more onerous parts of probate. They have created categories of property and beneficiaries that don't have to go through a full-blown probate court proceeding. If your family can take advantage of these procedures after your death, you may not need to worry too much about avoiding probate.

Almost every state has some kind of simplified (summary) probate or out-of-court transfer process for one or more of these categories:

Small estates. Most states offer streamlined probate court procedures for small estates; what qualifies as a small estate varies widely from state to state. In many states, even if your total estate is too large to qualify as a small estate, your heirs can still make use of the simplified procedures if the amount that actually goes through probate is under the limit.

Personal property. If the estate is small, many states also let people collect personal property (that's anything but real estate) they've inherited by filling out a sworn statement (affidavit) and giving it to the person who has the property. Typically, the beneficiary must also provide some kind of proof of his or her right to inherit, such as a death certificate and copy of the will.

Property left to the surviving spouse. In some states, if a surviving spouse inherits less than a certain amount of property, no probate is necessary.

RESOURCE

More information about avoiding probate. To learn more about saving your family the costs and hassles of probate, see *8 Ways to Avoid Probate*, by Mary Randolph (Nolo).

Reducing Estate Taxes

The federal estate tax is imposed after your death, on property you leave at your death. Because everyone is entitled to a large estate tax exemption, the tax affects only large estates, and only about 1% of Americans end up owing it.

The Future of the Federal Estate and Gift Tax

In 2001, Congress passed legislation repealing the estate tax—but not until 2010, and only for one year. Unless Congress votes to change the current law, the estate tax will return in 2011. (The exact dates and amounts are shown below.)

In recent years, the exemption amount has gone up, and the tax rates have gone down, meaning that fewer people than ever need to worry about estate tax. That's likely to continue, as Congress is almost sure to pass legislation reviving the estate tax—and sustaining the high exemption amount—before the current law expires.

When Congress repealed the estate tax, it did not repeal the federal gift tax, although it raised the exemption and lowered the maximum rate. The lifetime gift tax exemption is $1 million, and (unlike the estate tax exemption) will stay there. That means you can make a total of $1 million of taxable gifts before owing any federal gift tax.

Federal Estate and Gift Tax: 2009-2011			
Year of Death	Unified Estate/Gift Tax Exemption	Gift Tax Exemption	Highest Estate and Gift Tax Rate
2009	$3.5 million	$1 million	45%
2010	Estate tax repealed	$1 million	Top individual income tax rate (gift tax only)
2011	$1 million unless Congress extends repeal	$1 million	50% unless Congress extends repeal

State Estate and Inheritance Taxes

Even if your estate isn't big enough to owe federal estate tax, the state may still take a bite.

Estate tax. Until 2005, most states didn't impose their own estate tax; instead, they took a share of the federal estate tax paid by large estates. (This is called a "pick-up" or "sop" tax.) But the federal legislation that started the phase-out of the federal estate tax also took away the share of estate tax that states got to keep. To get back some of what they lost, some states are collecting tax from estates that aren't big enough to owe any federal tax. So far, almost half the states have changed their laws so they can keep collecting estate tax.

Inheritance tax. Some states impose a separate tax on a deceased person's property, called an inheritance tax. The tax rate depends on who inherits the property; usually, spouses and other close relatives pay nothing or at a low rate.

If you live in a state that imposes an estate or inheritance tax, there's not much you can do to avoid it, save moving to another state. For each state's rules, see *The Executor's Guide: Settling a Loved One's Estate or Trust*, by Mary Randolph (Nolo).

Ways to Reduce Federal Estate Taxes

Here are some tax-saving strategies you may want to consider. Each can be used alone or in combination with other methods.

The AB Living Trust

Couples who have a large combined estate and leave everything to each other may be in for a big estate tax bill on the death of the second spouse. For example, a husband and wife each write wills that leave all of their property to the other. When the husband dies, both estates are worth just less than the estate tax exemption, so no tax is due. However, when the widow dies, her estate (which now includes his estate) exceeds the exemption amount and the estate will pay much more federal estate tax than if the husband had left his property directly to children or other beneficiaries.

One way to avoid this problem, and also provide some income for the surviving spouse, is for each spouse to leave the other property in an AB trust—sometimes called a bypass trust or marital life estate trust. With this kind of trust, the income goes to the survivor during his or her life. The principal goes to the named beneficiaries—often the children—when the second spouse dies.

The tax break comes because the surviving spouse never legally owns the trust property, so the property isn't part of the survivor's estate. If the survivor had inherited the property outright, it would have been subject to estate tax at the survivor's death.

> **EXAMPLE:** Thomas and Maria, husband and wife, are in their mid-70s, and each has assets worth $1.9 million. Thomas dies in 2007, and Maria two years later. Here's the tax situation, with and without an AB trust:
>
> - **Without an AB trust.** Thomas leaves everything outright to Maria. No estate tax is assessed because the value of his estate is less than the exemption amount. But the size of Maria's estate rises to $3.8 million. At her death, all property in excess of the exempt amount in 2009, $3.5 million, is taxed.
> - **With an AB trust.** Thomas and Maria establish an AB trust, with the income to go to the survivor for life and the principal to the children at the survivor's death. When Thomas dies, his $1.9 million is not taxed because it's below the exempt amount. The value of Maria's estate remains at $1.9 million.
>
>   When Maria dies, $3.5 million can be left to anyone free of estate tax, so there is no estate tax liability on her $1.9 million, which goes to the children. The $1.9 million that Thomas left in trust also goes to the children; it isn't taxed, because it was below the exemption amount at Thomas's death. It isn't part of Maria's estate, because she is not considered the owner.

The main drawback of an AB trust is that it limits the surviving spouse's rights. The surviving spouse can, at the option of the trust creator, be given the right to spend trust principal for medical needs and other basic necessities. But in most cases, he or she receives only the income from the money or property placed in trust—or the use of the property if it is tangible, such as a house. He or she does not own it.

If you make an AB trust, you should first be sure that the surviving spouse will be financially and emotionally comfortable receiving only the income from the money or property placed in the trust, with the children (or others) as the actual owners of the property.

> **RESOURCE**
>
> **More information about AB Trusts.** To learn more about AB trusts, see *Make Your Own Living Trust*, by Denis Clifford (Nolo) or consult a knowledgeable estate planning lawyer.

Annual Tax-Exempt Gifts

If you don't need all your income and property to live on, making sizable gifts while you're alive can be a good way to reduce eventual federal estate taxes before that tax is repealed. Currently, only gifts larger than $13,000 made to one person or organization in one calendar year count toward the personal estate tax exemption. You can give smaller gifts tax-free.

> **EXAMPLE:** Allen and Julia give each of their two daughters $26,000 every year for four years. They have transferred $208,000 without becoming liable for gift tax.

Other Tax-Exempt Gifts

Other gifts are exempt regardless of amount, including:
- gifts between spouses who are U.S. citizens (gifts to spouses who are not U.S. citizens are exempt only up to $133,000 per year)
- gifts paid directly for medical bills or school tuition, and

- gifts to tax-exempt charitable organizations.

Charitable Trusts

If you want to make a big contribution to a charitable cause you care about—and at the same time cut your income taxes now and guarantee some income for life—then a charitable trust may be for you. They're not just for the very rich; you can contribute to a "pooled" charitable trust with as little as $5,000.

QTIPs and QDOTs

These trusts, known by their catchy acronyms (easier to say than Qualified Terminable Interest Property trust, you have to admit), are mainly used by married couples concerned about estate tax. A QTIP lets couples postpone paying estate tax until the second spouse's death, and also lock in, while both are still alive, who inherits the property at the second spouse's death. A QDOT is useful when a spouse who is not a U.S. citizen stands to inherit a large amount of property.

Life Insurance Trusts

Although the proceeds of a life insurance policy don't go through probate, they are included in your estate for federal estate tax purposes. You can reduce the tax bill by giving ownership of the policy to a life insurance trust (or to the beneficiary directly) at least three years before your death. But like other estate tax-saving strategies, this one will have to be reassessed in light of the planned estate tax repeal.

Using Trusts to Control Property

Most people are content to leave their property to their survivors outright, without trying to control what they do with it. However, there are times, especially for people with very large estates, when it can make sense to impose controls on what people can do with property you leave them. We discuss the most common situations here.

Children and Young Adults

Many people who leave property to children or young adults want to delay the age at which the beneficiaries will receive the property. You can set up this kind of property management in your will. See Chapter 6.

Second or Subsequent Marriages

Some people enter into second, third or fourth marriages unconcerned about estate planning. If each spouse has enough property of his or her own to live comfortably, there may be no need to combine assets and create the problems that can arise as a result. In such cases, the simplest solution is often to make a prenuptial agreement making it clear that separate property stays separate; then each can make an independent estate plan for that property.

But in many second or subsequent marriages, one or both spouses may feel conflicted about estate planning. On one hand, a surviving spouse may need the income from, or the use of, the other spouse's property to live comfortably. On the other hand, either spouse may want to provide an inheritance for children from a former marriage. This situation becomes even more complicated when a current spouse and children from a former marriage don't get along well.

One possible solution is to set up a trust—often called a "marital property control trust"—to try to balance the interests and needs of all concerned. Essentially, this type of trust gives the surviving spouse some use of or income from the trust property, then leaves the property outright to children from a prior marriage when the surviving spouse dies.

A marital property control trust is very different from an AB trust (discussed above) intended only to reduce estate taxes. With an AB trust, the surviving spouse is usually granted the maximum rights allowed under IRS rules to use trust property. In contrast, a marital property control trust is designed to protect the trust principal, so that most of it still exists when the surviving spouse dies.

Trusts like these are tricky, and you'll need an experienced lawyer to help you set one up. To learn more about the unique concerns of couples in second or subsequent marriages, and how to solve them, you might want to turn to Nolo's book, *Estate Planning for Blended Families: Providing for Your Spouse & Children in a Second Marriage*, by Richard E. Barnes.

Beneficiaries With Special Needs

A person with a physical or mental disability may not be able to handle property, no matter what age. The solution is often to establish a trust—called a "special needs trust"—to manage the property while preserving the beneficiary's eligibility for government benefits. You can learn more about this kind of trust by reading *Special Needs Trusts: Protect Your Child's Financial Future*, by Stephen Elias (Nolo).

Big Spenders

If you want to leave a substantial amount of property to someone who is known to be irresponsible with money, a good estate planning lawyer can help you establish what's known as a "spendthrift trust." In it, you can empower a trusted person or institution to dole out the money a little at a time.

Groups of Beneficiaries

For any number of reasons, you may want the exact division of your estate to be determined after your death, instead of directing the division in a will or trust.

The usual way to accomplish this is to create what is called a "sprinkling trust." Usually, the trust creator names the beneficiaries of the trust during life, but does not specify what share each is to receive. That is done by the trustee, after the creator dies, under whatever terms the trust dictates. Again, you'll need an experienced lawyer to set up this kind of trust.

SEE AN EXPERT

How to find a good lawyer. Many of the estate planning strategies discussed in this chapter require a lawyer's help. For tips on finding the expert you need, see Chapter 13.

If You Need More Help

Y ou probably won't need a lawyer's help to make your Quicken WillMaker will. But you may come up with questions about your particular situation that should be answered by an expert. This is especially likely if you have a very large estate, must plan for an incapacitated minor or have to deal with the assets of a good-sized small business. We highlight these and other "red flags" throughout the manual and program.

Learning More

If you've read most of this manual and started making your own will, you may know more about wills than a fair number of lawyers do. If you have questions that these materials don't address, you may want to consult some other self-help books or websites before you consult a pricey expert. It's often worth the money to pay a good lawyer for advice about your specific situation; it's rarely worth it to pay by the hour for education. Reading some background information before hiring a lawyer is usually the best approach.

Here are some Nolo books that provide more in-depth information about estate planning:

- *Plan Your Estate*, by Denis Clifford. This book explains how to draw up a complete estate plan making use of a will, living trust and other devices. It introduces more complex estate planning strategies, including various types of tax- saving trusts for the very wealthy.
- *8 Ways to Avoid Probate*, by Mary Randolph. If you're interested in learning more about some of the probate-avoidance techniques discussed in this manual, check out this book.
- *Make Your Own Living Trust,* by Denis Clifford. This bestselling book with CD-ROM shows you how to make the right living trust for your situation. Find it at www.nolo.com or through your favorite bookseller.
- *Estate Planning for Blended Families: Providing for Your Spouse & Children in a Second Marriage*, by Richard E. Barnes. This is the first book written for parents who want to provide both for

their current spouse and for their children from their current and prior marriages. It will help you identify your goals and put strategies in place to meet them.

- *Prenuptial Agreements: How to Write a Fair & Lasting Contract*, by Katherine E. Stoner and Shae Irving. Estate planning is often an important component of writing a prenuptial agreement. If you're planning to be married and considering a written agreement, this book will walk you through the process, including lots of guidance to help you communicate and negotiate a plan that will please both of you.

- *Special Needs Trusts: Protect Your Child's Financial Future*, by Stephen Elias. This book will help you understand and draft a trust to protect a disabled child. Even if you decide to have a lawyer draw up or finalize the trust, you will be armed with the information you need to get the best possible help.

- *The Executor's Guide: Settling a Loved One's Estate or Trust*, by Mary Randolph. This is an invaluable handbook for anyone asked to serve as an executor. It can also help you prepare your estate for your own executor, to make the job as easy as possible.

Nolo Blogs

Nolo's experts are now blogging about day-to-day legal issues that affect your life. For useful, and often entertaining, information about wills, trusts,and other estate planning issues, visit Nolo's Everyday Estate Planning Blog at www.estateplanninglawblawg.com.

What Kind of Expert Do You Need?

If you have questions, the first thing to decide is what type of expert you should seek. Questions about estate taxes may be better (and less expensively) answered by an experienced accountant than a lawyer. Or if you're wondering what type of life insurance to buy, you may be better off talking to a financial planner.

Consult a lawyer if you have specific questions about a provision of your will. Also see a lawyer if you want to get into more sophisticated estate planning—for instance, if you want to establish a charitable trust or a detailed plan to avoid estate taxes.

Different Ways to Get Advice From a Lawyer

Although many consumers (and some lawyers) don't know it yet, the way lawyers and their customers structure their relationships is changing fast. Lawyers used to insist on taking responsibility (and fees) for creating an entire estate plan. But, in what has become a very competitive market, many lawyers now offer piecemeal services, tailored to just what a customer wants.

This means you no longer have to walk into a lawyer's office, turn over your legal problems and wait for an answer—and a bill. Instead, you can often buy what you need, whether it's a bit of advice, a single estate planning document, a review of a document you've prepared with this program or regular coaching as you handle a probate court proceeding on your own.

If you adopt this approach, you and the lawyer should sign an agreement that clearly sets out your roles and states that the lawyer is not acting in a traditional role, but instead giving you limited services or representation. Without this type of agreement, lawyers fear that dissatisfied clients might later hold them responsible for more than they actually agreed to take on. The agreement should make things clear to you too, so you know what to expect from the lawyer. (For more, see "Working With a Lawyer," below.)

Finding a Lawyer

Finding a competent lawyer who charges a reasonable fee and respects your efforts to prepare your own estate planning documents may not be easy. First of all, you'll want to find a lawyer who specializes in estate planning. Most general practice lawyers are simply not sufficiently educated in this field to competently address complicated problems. Here are some other ways to look for help.

Personal Recommendations

The best way to find a lawyer is to get a recommendation from someone you trust. So ask your relatives and friends—especially those you know who have substantial assets and have likely made an estate plan. You may also want to ask those who run their own businesses. They are likely to have a relationship with a lawyer, and if that lawyer doesn't handle estate planning, he or she probably knows someone who does.

Finally, you might check with people you know in any social or other organization in which you are involved. Senior citizens' centers and other groups that advise and assist older people may have a list of local lawyers who specialize in wills and estate planning and are well regarded.

Group Legal Plans

Some unions, employers and consumer action organizations offer group legal plans to their members or employees, who can obtain legal assistance free or for low rates. If you are a member of such a plan, check with it first. Your problem may be covered free of charge. If it is, and you are satisfied that the lawyer you are referred to is knowledgeable in estate planning, this route is probably a good choice.

Some plans, however, give you only a slight reduction in a lawyer's fee. In that case, you may be referred to a lawyer whose main virtue is the willingness to reduce fees in exchange for a high volume of referrals. Chances are you can find a better lawyer outside the plan and negotiate a similar fee.

Attorney Directories

A lawyer directory will give you the names of attorneys who practice in your area. You will probably find several who specialize in estate planning and will give you an initial consultation for a low fee.

Following are two directories that may help you. Be sure to take the time to check out the credentials and experience of any lawyer who is listed.

Nolo's Lawyer Directory. Nolo offers a directory at lawyers.nolo. com that provides a detailed profile for each attorney with information to help you select the right lawyer for you. Attorneys use their profiles to describe their experience, education and fees and also to tell you something about the lawyer's general approach to practicing law. (For example, each lawyer states whether he or she is willing to review documents or coach clients who are doing their own legal work.) Nolo has confirmed that every listed attorney has a valid license and is in good standing with his or her local bar association.

West's Legal Directory. This directory lists most lawyers in the United States—more than 700,000 of them. You can look for a lawyer by location and legal practice category; there's a good chance you'll find more than one estate planning lawyer in your area. You can find the directory at lawyers.findlaw.com or in your local law library.

Attorney Referral Services

Your local county bar may have an attorney referral service, which differs from a directory in that a referral service will gather some information about your legal needs and match you with attorneys who might be a good fit for you. Usually you'll get only a few names of attorneys to consider, chosen for you by the knowledgeable people running the referral service, rather than having an entire directory to choose from on your own.

Working With a Lawyer

Before you talk to a lawyer, decide what kind of help you really need. Do you want someone to advise you on a complete estate plan, or just to review the documents you prepare to make sure they look all right? If you don't clearly tell the lawyer what you want, you may find yourself agreeing to turn over all your estate planning work.

One good strategy is to do some background research and write down your questions as specifically as you can. If the lawyer doesn't give you clear, concise answers, try someone else. If the lawyer acts wise but says little except to ask that the problem be placed in his or her hands—with a substantial fee, of course—watch out. You're either dealing with someone who doesn't know the answer and won't admit it (common) or someone who finds it impossible to let go of the "me expert, you plebeian" philosophy (even more common).

Lawyer fees usually range from $100 to $350 or more per hour. But price is not always related to quality. It depends on the area of the country you live in, but, generally, fees of $150 to $200 per hour are reasonable in urban areas. In rural areas and smaller cities, $100 to $150 is more like it. The fee of an experienced specialist may be 10% to 30% higher than that of a general practitioner, but the specialist will probably produce results more efficiently and save you money in the long run.

Be sure you settle your fee arrangement—preferably in writing—at the start of your relationship. In addition to the hourly fee, you should get a clear, written commitment from the lawyer about how many hours your problem should take to handle.

RESOURCE
For more information about working with lawyers and holding down legal fees, visit Nolo's Lawyer Directory at Nolo.com/lawyers/index.html. Click "working with Attorneys" to find helpful—and free—articles on the subject.

Doing Your Own Legal Research

There is often a viable alternative to hiring a lawyer to resolve legal questions that affect your estate planning documents: You can do your own legal research. Doing your own legal research can provide some real benefits if you are willing to learn how to do it. Not only will you save some money, you will gain a sense of mastery over an area of law, generating confidence that will stand you in good stead should you have other legal problems.

Fortunately, researching wills and related estate planning issues is an area generally well suited to doing your own legal research. Most problems do not involve massive or abstruse legal questions. Often you need only check the statutes of your state to find one particular provision.

RESOURCE

Nolo's website, www.nolo.com, offers a section on estate planning that covers a range of topics including living trusts and estate and gift taxes. You can also find links to state and federal statutes from the site.

Legal Research: How to Find & Understand the Law, by Stephen Elias and Susan Levinkind (Nolo), gives instructions and examples explaining how to conduct legal research.

Finding Statutes in a Law Library

You can always find state statutes at a law library or, usually, at the main branch of a public library. Depending on the state, statutes are compiled in books called statutes, revised statutes, annotated statutes, codes or compiled laws. For example, the Vermont statutes are found in a series called *Vermont Statutes Annotated,* while Michigan's laws are found in two separate sets of books: *Michigan Statutes* or an alternate series called *Michigan Compiled Laws.* (The term "annotated" means that the statutes are accompanied by information about their history and court decisions that have interpreted them.) The reference librarian can point you toward the books you need.

After you've found the books, check the index for provisions dealing with the specific subject that concerns you—for example, wills. Generally, you will find what you want in the volume of statutes dealing with your state's basic civil or probate laws. Statutes are numbered sequentially, so once you get the correct number in the index, it will be easy to find the statute you need.

Once you find a law in the statute books, it's important to look at the update pamphlet in the back of the book (called the "pocket part") to make sure your statute hasn't changed or been repealed. Pocket parts are published only once per year, so brand-new laws often have not yet made it to the pocket part. Law libraries subscribe to services and periodicals that update the statute books on a more frequent basis than the pocket parts. You can ask a law librarian to help you find the materials you need.

Finally, you may find summaries of relevant court cases immediately following the statute. (These are the annotations mentioned just above.) If so, you'll want to skim them. If a summary looks like it might help answer your question, read the full court case cited there. (Ask the librarian for help finding the case, or turn to the legal research resource listed above.)

Finding Statutes Online

All states have made their statutes available on the Internet. You can find them by visiting the legal research area of Nolo's website at www.nolo.com/legal-research. Choose your state to search or browse the statutes.

In addition, almost every state maintains its own website for pending and recently enacted legislation. If you hear about a proposed or new law and you want to look it up, you can use your state's website to find not only the most current version of a bill, but also its history. To find your state's website, open your browser and type in www.state.[your state's postal code].us. Your state's postal code is the two-letter abbreviation you use for mailing addresses. For example, NY is the postal code for New York, so to find New York's state website, type www.state.ny.us. When you open your state's home page, look for links under "government." All states have separate links to their legislatures, and they offer many different ways to look up bills and laws. You can also find any state's legislature through the National Conference of State Legislatures at www.ncsl.org.

Users' Manual Table of Contents

Appendixes

A Menu Options

B Keyboard Shortcuts

C Error Messages

Getting the Most Out of Quicken WillMaker

Welcome to Quicken WillMaker 2010. Quicken WillMaker makes it easy for you and your immediate family to create wills and leave information for caregivers and survivors.

You don't need legal training or estate planning experience to create a will with Quicken WillMaker. The onscreen interview provides easy-to-understand guidance every step of the way. And if you need more help than you see onscreen, the two product manuals are just a click away:

- This Users' Manual explains how to use the program.
- The Legal Manual provides legal and practical answers to help you create your documents.

You can view electronic versions of both manuals at any time from within Quicken WillMaker. Many screens have links that take you directly to the sections of the manuals that relate to the question you're answering.

This part of the Users' Manual gives you a preview of how the program works, along with some tips for using it to your best advantage.

How Quicken WillMaker Works

Two points are key to understanding Quicken WillMaker:

- The program interviews you and uses your answers to create documents.
- Much of the document-creation work happens invisibly, behind the scenes.

Interview at Your Own Pace

Each document you can create with Quicken WillMaker has its own interview. You click through the questions and answer them at your own pace.

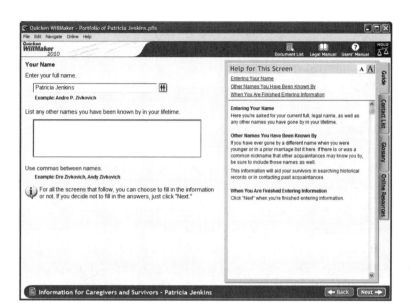

When you finish an interview, the program combines your answers with the appropriate legal language and displays the completed document for you to review.

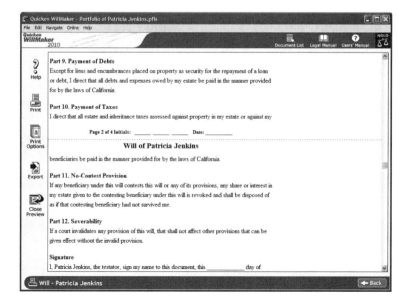

Unlike some other programs, you don't type directly into Quicken WillMaker documents or edit their language. This safeguard ensures that the documents use the exact language needed to make them legally valid. When you need to make changes to a document, you go back to the appropriate sections of the document interview and change your answers there.

Because Quicken WillMaker customizes later interview questions based on the answers you give to earlier ones, a changed answer may affect the rest of your interview—so after you make a change to a document you may be asked to go back and review some (or all) of the interview questions you've already answered.

You can produce any document in Quicken WillMaker in one sitting, but there's no point in rushing. Relax and take your time—after all, Quicken WillMaker doesn't charge by the hour. Read the "Help for This Screen" section of the onscreen Guide and consider it thoughtfully. You can always stop a document interview and come back later; it's easy to pick up exactly where you left off.

When you're satisfied with your document, print and sign it, following the signing instructions that we provide. These instructions tell you how to finalize your document and make it legal.

Looking Behind the Scenes

Part of what makes Quicken WillMaker easy to use is the work the program does invisibly, without your noticing. For example, when you type in a person's name, the program automatically creates an entry for that person in the Contact List section of the program, where contact information is stored for reuse.

While you can get along fine without knowing most of what Quicken WillMaker is doing behind the scenes, learning a little about what's happening in the background can help you use the program more efficiently and effectively. This manual's "Behind the Scenes" features alert you to actions the program is taking and tell you how they may affect you. Look for the "Behind the Scenes" icon shown below:

Read these notes to become a "power user" of Quicken WillMaker.

Getting Started

t's easy to start using Quicken WillMaker. Typically, you'll need to:

1. Install Quicken WillMaker.
2. Start the program.
3. Register your copy of the program.
4. Update your version of the program.
5. Get oriented to the screen elements.
6. Begin creating your will or information for caregivers and survivors form.

Steps 3 through 5 are optional, but we strongly recommend that you go through them all—especially Step 4, which ensures that you are using the most up-to-date version of the program.

This part of the manual takes you through all of the above steps except creating documents; you'll read about that in Part 3.

Making Sure Your System Meets the Requirements

Before you install Quicken WillMaker, check that your system meets these minimum requirements:

- **Computer.** Pentium 400 MHz
- **Operating System.** Windows *XP/Vista*
- **Memory.** 512 MB RAM
- **Hard Disk Space.** 16 MB (23 MB to install)
- **Monitor.** Super 1024 x 768 with 16-bit color
- **CD-ROM Drive.** 2x speed
- **Internet Connection.** 56 Kbps required to access online features
- **Printer.** Any printer supported by Windows *XP/Vista*
- **Software.** Microsoft *Internet Explorer* 6.0 or higher; Adobe *Reader* (optional).

Installing Quicken WillMaker

You install Quicken WillMaker by running the installer. Here's how:

1. Insert the Quicken WillMaker disc into your CD-ROM drive to launch the automatic setup program. If the automatic setup program doesn't launch automatically when you insert the Quicken WillMaker CD, see "Jump-Starting the Setup Program" in Part 7.
2. Follow the instructions that appear on screen to complete installation. If you're prompted to restart your computer after installation, do so.

SKIP AHEAD

Skip ahead if your installation is now complete. If you need more information to help you perform the above steps, see the discussions just below. If not, skip ahead to "Starting Quicken WillMaker."

Checking Out the Program Folder

Before using your newly installed version of Quicken WillMaker, we suggest you take a look at the information in the **Quicken WillMaker 2010** program folder on your hard drive.

To open the program folder and check out its contents, follow these steps:

1. From the Windows taskbar, choose **Start > Programs** (or **All Programs**) **> Quicken WillMaker 2010**.
2. Click **Troubleshooting** to open the file and skim its contents. It contains late-breaking and situation-specific information for troubleshooting or preventing problems.

Starting Quicken WillMaker

You can start the program in either of the following ways:
- by double-clicking the Quicken WillMaker icon on your desktop (if you chose this option during installation), or
- by choosing (from the Windows taskbar) **Start > Programs** (or **All Programs**) **> Quicken WillMaker 2010** (folder) **> Quicken WillMaker 2010** (program).

The first time you use the program, you won't go straight to the Document List. Instead, you'll encounter an introductory, "Welcome to Quicken WillMaker" screen, followed by a screen inviting you to use the Web Update feature.

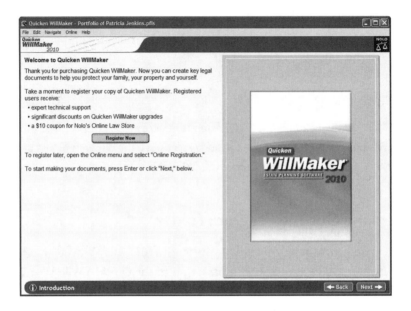

If you like, you can come back to these screens later by choosing **Navigate > Go to Introduction**.

Registering Your Copy of the Program

Registering your copy of Quicken WillMaker gives you access to a variety of services and benefits, including technical support. We recommend that you register as soon as you start up the program.

To register your copy:

1. Do one of the following:

    - From the "Welcome to Quicken WillMaker" screen, click **Register Now**.

- From anyplace else in the program, choose **Online > Online Registration**.

2. Follow the directions on the online registration page.

If you don't have an Internet connection, look in the back of your printed manual for a registration card that you can fill out and send in.

Updating Your Version of the Program

Because software boxes sometimes sit on shelves for a while, the version of Quicken WillMaker that you bought may not be the most current. We regularly update the program to accommodate changing laws or fix problems our users report. To make sure you're running the latest version, use Web Update, a feature that downloads and installs any revisions we've made to the program.

Run Web Update the first time you use the program and as often as possible thereafter—either automatically at program startup (the default preference for the program) or manually at intervals you choose.

Running Web Update Manually

To run Web Update manually:

1. Do one of the following:
   - From the "Keep Quicken WillMaker Up to Date" screen in the program's introduction, click **Web Update**.
   - From anyplace else in the program, choose **Online > Web Update**.

2. Follow the directions that appear on screen.

TIP
If you have Internet connection problems. If you're having trouble connecting to the Internet from within Quicken WillMaker, open your Web browser as you normally would from outside the program, then return to the program and try again. If problems persist, see "Handling Web Update Problems" in Part 7.

Enabling and Disabling Automatic Updates

By default, Quicken WillMaker checks for newer versions every time you start up the program (as long as you have an open Internet connection). If it detects a newer version, you're prompted to download and install the newer files (which may take a few minutes). The program will then restart.

If you'd rather not have these checks done automatically, you can turn off this feature by changing the default preference. If you decide to change this preference—we recommend that you don't—be sure to run Web Update manually at regular intervals.

To change the "automatic update" preference:

1. Choose **Edit > Preferences**.
2. Click the check box next to **Automatically check for updates when the program starts** to mark it with a ✔—or to clear the ✔ from the box if it's already checked. If the check box is empty, the program will check for updates only when you run Web Update manually.

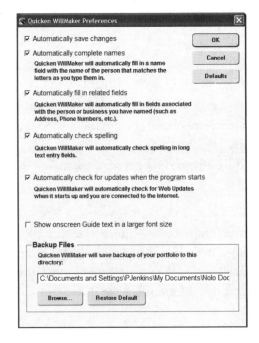

Getting Oriented

The program's general screen layout makes everything you need obvious:

- The onscreen Guide is right up front, providing plenty of basic information to help you understand the current task and answer any questions you may have about it.
- The **Next** button at the bottom of the screen clearly points you to your next task.
- If you want to take a detour or a break before going to the next task, you can click the **Back** button or choose from a variety of menu and navigation options at the top of the screen. (If you're not sure what a particular menu command means, see the descriptions in Appendix A.)

When you start creating documents, you'll encounter a wider variety of onscreen options (explained in Part 3), but for now, the options explained here should be pretty much all you need to know.

Quitting and Restarting Quicken WillMaker

You can quit Quicken WillMaker by doing any of the following:

- Choose **File > Exit**.
- Click the close box (marked with an "X") in the upper right-hand corner of the program.
- Press ALT+F4.

Any changes you've made to your documents since the last time you saved your data are automatically saved when you quit. By default, the **Automatically save changes** feature is turned on. If you've turned **Automatically save changes** off (in **Edit > Preferences**) the programs prompts you to save your changes when you quit. For more information on saving your data, see "Saving Your Portfolio" in Part 5.

You can restart the program just as you started it the first time, either from the Windows taskbar or by double-clicking the program's icon on your desktop. If you completed the program's introduction before you quit, you'll go directly to the Document List. The Document

List is your main jumping-off point for creating documents (or for working with documents you've already created)—and you'll find out all about it in Part 3.

Creating Documents

C reating documents with Quicken WillMaker is simple: You answer the interview questions and when you've finished the interview, the program generates the document for you, with all the legal niceties in place.

This part of the Users' Manual orients you to the Document List (where you choose a document to work on) and describes how to start, proceed through and complete document interviews.

Exploring the Document List

The Document List in Quicken WillMaker is your home base in the program, similar to the home page for a website. It's the screen you see when you start the program (unless you haven't yet viewed the introductory screens discussed in Part 2). You can easily get to the Document List from most other parts of the program.

Navigating to the Document List

To get to the Document List:
- on the navigation bar, click **Document List**, or
- choose **Navigate > Go to Document List**.

At the Document List, you can view all your document options, have the program suggest documents, choose a document to work on and launch its interview. But first, you should get oriented to the Document List screen and its elements.

Getting Oriented to the Document List

The Document List includes the following elements:

① List of Document Names

This list shows the name of documents you can create (Will and Information for Caregivers and Survivors), as well as all of the documents you created.

② Create/Open Document Button

Click this button after you've selected the template or document you want to work on. The name of the button changes depending on whether the document name you've selected represents a template or an actual document:

- If you've selected a template name, the button is **Create Document**.
- If you've selected the name of an already created document, the button is **Open Document**.

③ Description of Selected Document or Category

When you click "Will" or "Information for Caregivers and Survivors," the text to the right describes the document you've selected. This description includes a link to a sample document, so you can see what a finished version looks like.

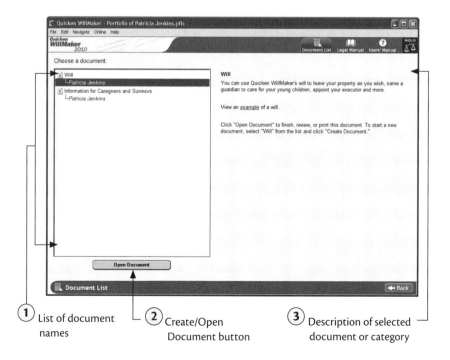

> **BEHIND THE SCENES**
>
> **Many documents, one portfolio file.** Quicken WillMaker saves all the documents you create in one portfolio file, which also contains the contact information you enter in your Contact List. The file is named "Portfolio of [*Your Name*].pfls" using the name you entered during the program's introduction.
>
> This "one file" approach allows Quicken WillMaker documents to share contact information and saves you time. (You don't need to reenter names and addresses when you refer to the same people in multiple documents.) Plus, you can change contact information easily in one place—the Contact List (described in Part 6)—and let the program extend the changes to all relevant documents.
>
> To find out more about portfolio files and how to use them to manage your documents, see Part 5.

Starting Your Document

The first step in creating a new document in Quicken WillMaker is selecting the document interview. You can create a completely new document or make a different version of a document you've already created.

Starting a Completely New Document

To start a completely new document:

1. Go to the Document List (if you aren't already there) by clicking **Document List** on the navigation bar.
2. Choose a category of documents from the drop-down category list.
3. Select the name (in black type) of the document you want to create. (Remember, names in black type represent document templates, while names in blue type represent documents already created.)
4. Click **Create Document**.

The first screen of your document interview appears. See "Using Checklists for Interview Management," below, for tips about using the checklist to navigate an interview and monitor your progress. Simply proceed through the interview screens in order and supply the requested information.

> **BEHIND THE SCENES**
> **Know when your document is actually created.** Clicking **Create Document** starts the interview process, but the program doesn't actually create your document until you enter some information on an interview screen and save it by moving on to the next screen. If you were to select a document and read only an introductory interview screen, you haven't created that document.

Creating an Identical Will for a Spouse or Partner

> **SKIP AHEAD**
> **If you aren't married or partnered.** You can skip this section if you aren't married or in a domestic partnership.

Some married couples or couples in a domestic partnership may want to create identical wills, where all the provisions in the will—such as beneficiaries, alternate beneficiaries and children's guardians—are the same, except that the spouses' or partners' names are reversed. For example, if you make a will and name your spouse or partner as your executor, the identical will for your spouse or partner will name you as your spouse's or partner's executor.

Married couples or partners are not required to create identical wills. But for those who want to do so, Quicken WillMaker offers a feature specifically for this purpose.

TIP

Work on the will interview together. Because the first spouse or partner to write a will is in effect creating the will for both of you, we suggest that the two of you complete the will interview together, discussing and agreeing to all decisions and choices.

When you have completed the will for one spouse or partner, here's how to duplicate it for the other:

1. Go to the "Congratulations" screen for the will of the first spouse or partner. (See "Getting to the 'Congratulations' Screen" in Part 4.)

2. Click **Duplicate for Spouse**.

3. The Document List appears after you read an advisory dialog box and click **OK**. The duplicated will appears on the list with the status description "in progress."

4. Double-click the duplicated will (or select it and click the **Open Document** button).

5. The checklist for the duplicated will appears after you read an advisory dialog box and click **OK**. Note that none of the parts on this checklist are checked, even though this will contains the information carried over from the first will; these parts will be checked when you have reviewed the information.

6. For each part in the checklist, click through all interview screens to make sure the second spouse or partner agrees with the choices the first one has made. You can change the information in this will, but keep in mind that these changes will not be reflected in the will of the first will-writing spouse or partner.

7. When you've reviewed all screens, you can preview and print the completed will as described in Part 4.

Proceeding Through an Interview

Once you start the interview for the document you selected, all you have to do is click through the screens in the interview and supply the information needed to correctly generate it.

This section of the manual shows you how to navigate through an interview using the various data entry formats you may encounter along the way.

Read each interview question carefully and consult the program's help resources (the onscreen Guide, the Legal Manual and this Users' Manual) to help you decide on your answers. (For more information about help resources and how to access them, see "Getting Oriented" in Part 2, or read Part 7, "Getting Help.")

Moving Forward

To move to the next screen in an interview, use any of the following methods:

- Click **Next**.
- Choose **Navigate > Next**.
- Press ALT+RIGHT ARROW.
- Use the TAB key to move the keyboard focus to the **Next** button, then press the ENTER key or the SPACEBAR. (The keyboard focus is on a button when a dotted outline surrounds the button.)

If the information requested on the current screen is optional, you can go on to the next screen without supplying the information. However, if the information is required, the program won't let you move to the next screen without answering.

If you're not sure how to answer, we suggest you quit the interview and return to it later; when you return, the interview will pick up where you left off. Or, you can give a placeholder answer and move on—but if you do so, you may need to come back and change several answers later, because later parts of the interview may be determined by your answer.

Moving Backward

To go back to the previous screen in an interview, use any of the following methods:

- Click **Back**.
- Choose **Navigate > Back**.
- Press ALT+LEFT ARROW.
- Use the TAB key to move the keyboard focus to the **Back** button, then press the ENTER key or the SPACEBAR. (The keyboard focus is on a button when a dotted outline surrounds the button.)

> ⓘ CAUTION
>
> **Don't lose data when you backtrack.** Quicken WillMaker may not record what you've entered on the current screen until you move to the next screen. If you enter or change an answer and then try to go back to the previous screen, the program will warn you if your answer or change won't be saved. To save your answer before backtracking, first click **Next** to move one screen forward; then back up to previous screens.

You have an additional method for going backward: Use the checklist to reopen sections of the interview you've already completed. To find out more about checklists, see "Using Checklists for Interview Management," below.

Revising Answers You've Entered

Because Quicken WillMaker sometimes chooses interview questions based on your answers to earlier questions, revising one answer may affect everything that comes after it. So, after you go back to revise a recent answer (using any of the methods described in "Moving Backward," above), you'll need to continue going forward, one screen at a time, making any necessary corrections. Use the checklist to reopen the section of the interview that contains the answer you want to change; then click forward through that entire section, making changes as needed. (See "Using Checklists for Interview Management," below.)

Using Checklists for Interview Management

When you start a document in Quicken WillMaker, the first screen is the interview checklist. This checklist provides an overview of the parts of the interview, so you know which topic is covered in each part.

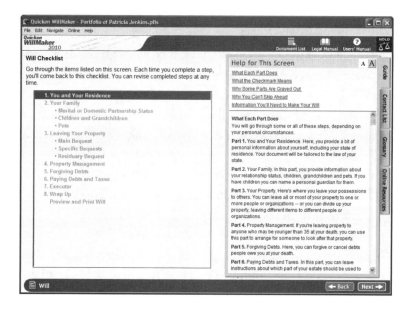

The checklist helps to keep track of which parts of an interview you've completed and simplifies the process of going back to change an answer. Rather than stepping through the whole interview, you can go directly to the part you want to change.

Understanding Checkmarks and Dimmed List Items

The checkmarks on a checklist show which parts of the interview you have completed. Dimmed items are unavailable for you to work on.

List items are dimmed:

- to prevent you from working on interview parts out of order, or
- to prevent you from working on interview parts that aren't relevant to your situation.

Quicken WillMaker determines which parts of the interview don't apply to you based on the answers you've given to previous questions. For example, in the will interview, if you say in "2. Children and Grandchildren" that you don't have kids, then "4. Property Management for Children" is dimmed because it's not relevant to your situation.

Working on Document Parts

When you are working on a will, you must go through the interview parts in order. However, you can return to previously completed parts (parts with checkmarks) in any order.

However, in the information for caregivers and survivors form, after completing the introduction, you can work on the remaining parts in any order you wish.

To work on a document part listed in the checklist:

1. Select the name of the document part in the checklist.
2. Click **Next** (or use any other method of forward movement described in "Moving Forward," above).

The first screen in the selected part of the interview appears. If you have selected **Preview and Print,** you will go directly to the "Congratulations" screen. There you can preview, print or export your document. (For more information about performing these tasks, see Part 4.)

Answering Interview Questions

A Quicken WillMaker interview will ask you to supply information in the following ways:

- typing into text-entry boxes
- using icons to select names and dates
- adding items to list boxes
- choosing radio-button options
- choosing check-box options
- selecting from pick lists, and
- selecting from drop-down lists.

This section explains how to use each of these formats. For instructions on how to answer specific interview questions, consult the Guide on the right side of each interview screen.

As you proceed through the interview, keep in mind that the program doesn't save the information you enter on a given screen until you move forward to the next one.

BEHIND THE SCENES

Some questions are answered automatically. On some interview screens, you may find answers already filled in with information, such as the address or phone number for a person or organization. Quicken WillMaker finds this information, which you entered previously, in your Contact List and automatically inserts it for you. If you revise automatically inserted information on the interview screen, it will also be revised in the Contact List and in all documents that use this information.

Typing Into Text-Entry Boxes

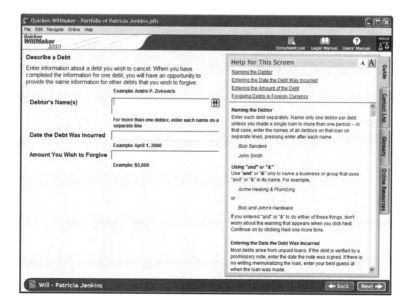

On some screens, you type information—such as a name, address, fraction, date or description of an item of property—in a text-entry box. (If you can't type into the box and you see an **Add to List** button on the same screen, the box is actually a list box; see "Adding Items to List Boxes," below.)

Most text-entry boxes hold a single answer to an interview question. However, you will also encounter text-entry boxes in which you can enter multiple names or other items on separate lines.

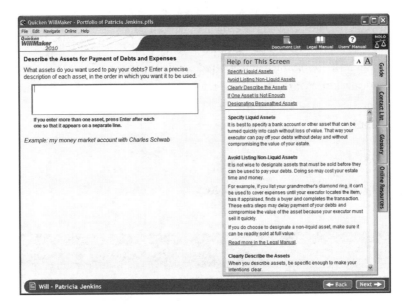

Both types of text-entry box require the same basic steps:

1. If the text-entry box doesn't have a blinking cursor in it, click in the box or press the TAB key as needed to put the cursor in the box.

2. Type in your answer (or click the **Insert Name From Contact List** or **Select a Date** icon next to the box, if applicable). When appropriate, refer to the example below the box to see how to format your answer. If you're entering a name, see "Tips for Entering Names," below, for some useful advice.

Tips for Entering Names

Because a name used in one part document interview may appear again in that document (or in others), Quicken WillMaker Plus keeps track of all the names you enter and stores them in your Contact List.

Using this list, the program checks your answers for logical inconsistencies and alerts you if a name entered in one place can't be used there based on answers you've given earlier.

To enable Quicken WillMaker Plus to perform its error checking correctly, and keep your Contact List as accurate as possible, follow these tips when entering names:

- Use full names, first name first.
- Be consistent: Use the same exact name for a person or organization throughout the document interview. If you use a full name in one answer and a nickname in another, the program will assume they are different and add both to the Contact List.
- Carefully check the spelling of all names before you leave the screen. The program assumes different spellings are different people and adds both names to the Contact List.
- If the program fills in a name automatically after you've typed in a few characters (guessing that it is a name from your Contact List), check that it truly is the name you want to enter. If it isn't, continue typing the correct name. (To turn off the "automatic completion" feature, choose **Edit > Preferences**.)
- Enter only one name per line. To begin a new line for an additional name, follow the onscreen instructions.
- Whenever possible, use the Contact List to paste in names that you've entered previously, as described in "Pasting in Contact List Names," above.

If you discover you entered a name incorrectly and want to change it, choose **Edit > Manage Contact List** to correct the name in the Contact List; the program will make the correction in all documents where the name occurs. To find out more about working with the Contact List, see Part 6.

3. If the box is a text-entry box that allows multiple items to be entered and you want to type in another item, press Enter to start a new line and return to Step 2.

4. Proofread and spell check (see below) your data before proceeding to the next screen.

> **TIP**
> **Double-check formatting—especially of phone numbers and zip codes.** While Quicken WillMaker checks some data for correct formatting, telephone numbers and zip codes aren't checked (to allow for international contact data, phone extensions and so on). Be sure to review the format of your answer before moving to the next screen.

> **CAUTION**
> **Watch out for automatic ENTER-key navigation.** On most interview screens, pressing the ENTER key triggers the default navigation button, which is usually the **Next** button. If you are in the habit of pressing ENTER after you type in an answer, you may find yourself jumping to the next screen unintentionally. Remember, the only time you need to press ENTER while typing in data is if you want to start a new line in a text box that allows multiple items. (Pressing ENTER at other times will probably send you to the next screen.)

Using Icons to Select a Name or Date

To save you from retyping information, the program includes some shortcuts for entering names and dates.

Pasting in Contact List Names

When the answer to an interview question is a name that is already in your Contact List, you can avoid retyping it by pasting it in from your Contact List. The **Contact List** icon, which looks like a notepad page with two people on it, appears next to text-entry boxes where a name is requested.

To paste a Contact List name into a text-entry box:
1. Click the **Contact List** icon next to the text-entry box in which you want to paste the name.
2. Select the name you want to paste by clicking it.

If you are pasting multiple names from your Contact List into a text-entry box that allows multiple entries, you can either select and paste the names individually or use the **Select Multiple Names** feature.

To find out more about the Contact List, including how to edit contact information, see Part 6.

Selecting Dates

When the answer to an interview question is a date, you can use the **Select a Date** calendar icon, which appears next to text-entry boxes where dates are requested.

To insert a date into a text-entry box:
1. Click the **Select a Date** icon next to the text-entry box in which you want to enter a date. This opens a calendar below the date-entry box, with today's date already selected.
2. What happens next depends on what date you want to insert:
   - If you want to insert today's date, click on the day on the calendar.
   - If you want to insert a different date:
     • To change the year of the selected date, click the year, then use the arrows that appear to the right of the year.
     • To change the month of the selected date, use the arrows to the left and right of today's month and year.
     • To change the day of the selected month and year, click on the day you want to use.

Checking Your Spelling

You can make sure that the spelling of your answers to interview questions is correct using Quicken WillMaker's built-in spell checker. Here's how:

1. Type in your answer, as described in "Typing Into Text-Entry Boxes," above.

2. If, after you type a word, it turns red and is underlined, the program has identified it as a word that isn't in the program's dictionary.

3. Right click on the red word. A list of suggested words will come up. If you'd like to keep your word and add it to the dictionary, click Ignore All. If you'd like to select one of the alternates, click it.

Note: If you'd like to turn off the automatic spell check feature, choose **Edit > Preferences** and click the checkbox next to **Automatically check spelling**. This will uncheck the box and turn off the feature.

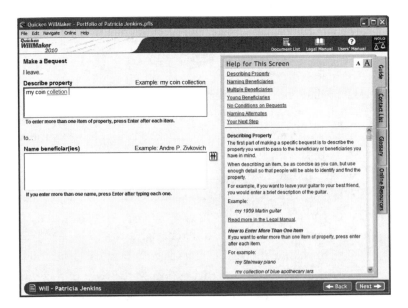

Adding Items to List Boxes

On some interview screens, you'll need to enter items in a list box and provide additional information about each listed item. For example, the will interview asks you to list each of your children and provide each child's gender and date of birth.

When you encounter an empty list box, the keyboard focus is on the button for adding list items, making this button the default choice.

Each screen with a list box contains detailed instructions on how to use its particular list, but all use the same basic steps.

To add an item to a list box:

1. Click **Add to List**. (In some cases, the name of this button may be customized to reflect items contained in the list, for example, **Add a Child**.)
2. Answer whatever questions appear about the item you're adding.
3. Click **Next** or **OK** to return to the screen with the list box.

Once you've added all your items to the list, you can use the **Change** and **Remove** buttons as needed to change or remove selected items.

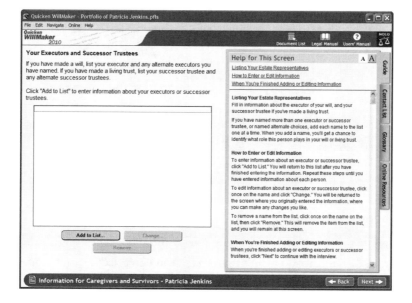

Choosing a Radio-Button Option

Some interview questions require you to choose one answer from several options using a list with radio buttons. When you click one radio button to select its option, any previous selection is erased. The selected option is the one with the black dot in the center of the button.

To choose a radio-button option:

- Click the radio button next to the option or use the ARROW keys on your keyboard to select it.

If an option is already selected when the screen appears, make sure it's the answer you want to give. If it isn't, choose a different option before you move on to the next screen.

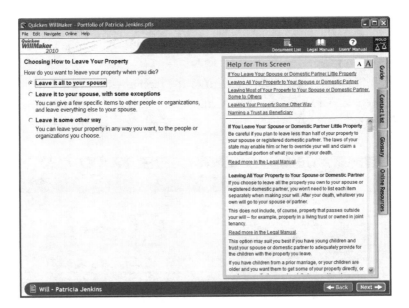

Choosing Check-Box Options

If a question requires you to choose one or more options from a list, the program displays a list with check boxes. You can select as many options from the list as you need.

To choose a check-box option:

- Click the check box next to the option to mark it with a ✔ (or use the TAB key to select the option, then press the SPACEBAR to mark the box with a ✔).

To remove a ✔ from a check box:

- Click the check box to clear it (or use the TAB key to select the option, then press the SPACEBAR to clear the ✔ from the check box).

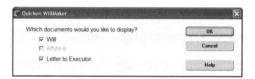

When you've made sure that only the options you want are checked, you can move on to the next screen.

Selecting From a Pick List

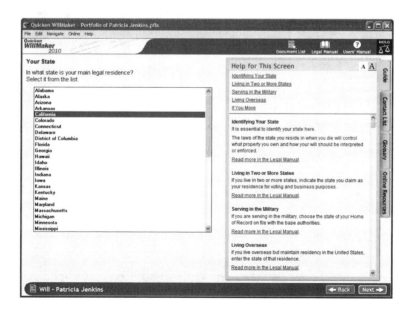

Some interview screens with long lists of selection options—such as a list of all the states in the United States—require you to choose one answer from a pick list.

To choose an option from a pick list:

1. Use the scroll bar or ARROW keys to see the entire list, if necessary (or type a letter to move the selection bar to the first list item that begins with that letter).

2. Click the option you want to select (or use the ARROW keys to select it).

Selecting From a Drop-Down List

Some interview questions require you to choose one answer from a drop-down list.

To choose an option from a drop-down list:

1. Click the arrow to the right of the list space to display a list box below the space. Use the scroll bar or ARROW keys to see the entire list, if needed.

2. Click the option you want to select.

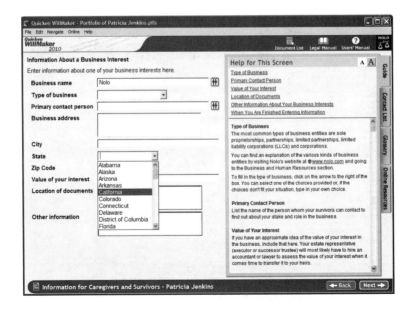

Stopping and Restarting Your Interview

You can stop an interview in progress at any time, either by quitting the program or by navigating to another part of the program—for example, clicking the **Document List** icon to return to the Document List.

When you select the name of a document that was not completed in the Document List, the status line below the list shows the document's creation date and the description "in progress."

Saving Your Data

Quicken WillMaker automatically saves the information you provide on an interview screen when you move on to the next one (unless you've turned off the **Automatically save changes** feature in the program preferences), so you generally don't need to worry about saving data. The program saves all of your documents and contact information in your portfolio. (Portfolios are explained in Part 5.)

If you have turned off the **Automatically save changes** feature in the program preferences, you'll need to save data manually at frequent intervals. The program asks if you want to save changes whenever you quit.

To save data manually:

- Choose **File > Save**.

To change your preference for the **Automatically save changes** feature:

1. Choose **Edit > Preferences** to open the **Preferences** dialog box.
2. Click the check box next to **Automatically save changes** to turn this feature on if it's off (or off if it's on). A check mark (✔) indicates the option is on.

We strongly recommend you leave this feature on.

For more information on saving and backing up your data, see Part 5.

Completing Your Interview

When you've completed all the interview screens, the program has all the information it needs to assemble and print your document. The next step takes you to the "Congratulations" screen, which lets you view, print, revise and export your document. This screen appears automatically when you complete the interview—unless the interview for your document uses a checklist, in which case you need to select **Preview and Print** from the checklist, then click the **Next** button.

To learn more about working with your completed document, see Part 4.

Reviewing, Changing and Printing Your Documents

A fter you've completed your document interview, Quicken WillMaker uses your answers to create a finished document. The "Congratulations" screen, which appears at the end of each interview, lets you look at the document and make any necessary changes before you print it out.

This part of the Users' Manual explains how to get to the "Congratulations" screen and use its options to review, change and print your document. It also discusses how to export your document to a text file.

SKIP AHEAD

This part of the manual doesn't cover how to print contact information or help topics. To find out about printing your Contact List, see "Printing Your Contact List" in Part 6. To learn about printing topics from the onscreen Guide or online manuals, see Part 7.

Getting to the "Congratulations" Screen

You can reach the "Congratulations" screen from the checklist after you've completed all required parts of the document. Double-click **Preview and Print** at the bottom of the checklist (or select **Preview and Print** and click **Next**).

The "Congratulations" screen provides options for previewing and printing your document, changing your answers and returning to the Document List.

TIP

Special option for will writers. For wills, the "Congratulations" screen also provides a **Duplicate for Spouse** button, which you can use to create an identical copy of the will for your spouse or partner. (For more information about this process, see "Creating an Identical Will for a Spouse or Partner" in Part 3.)

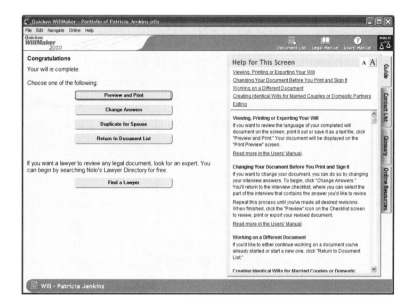

Reviewing Your Document in Print Preview

We recommend that you use Print Preview to carefully review your finished document. If you want to change any of your answers, you can do so before you print your document.

> ⓘ **CAUTION**
>
> **Signing instructions not included in Print Preview.** In addition to your document, each interview produces a set of related pages, including instructions on how to sign your document and make it legal. These signing instructions, and any additional pages, print out with the document (if you specify so in the **Print** dialog box) but they don't appear in Print Preview. Also, the format of the printed document (line breaks, page breaks and number of pages) may slightly differ in format from the version you see on screen.

To review your completed document:

1. Go to the "Congratulations" screen (see "Getting to the 'Congratulations' Screen," above), if you aren't already there.

2. Click **Preview and Print** to open the document preview.

3. You'll see a dialog box asking which specific documents in the document set you would like to display. If you don't want to display all of them, uncheck the ones you don't want before clicking **OK** (but be sure to include all of them when you print out the version you intend to sign and make legal).

4. In the document preview, use the scroll bar or press the UP and DOWN ARROW keys to move through the document and read it carefully, making sure the information is correct. (If you're curious about the hash marks ("////") that appear at the end of some pages, see the "Behind the Scenes" note, below.)

5. If you're not ready to print or export the document, click **Close Preview** on the left side of the document to return to the "Congratulations" screen.

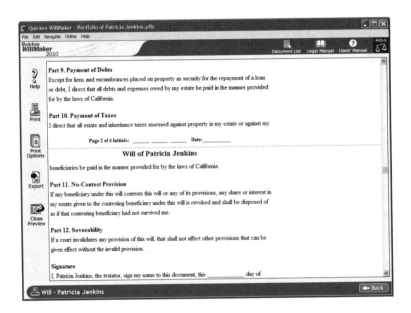

BEHIND THE SCENES

Those "////" marks on your document are there for a reason.
Quicken WillMaker uses "////"—also known as "hash marks"—in its printed documents as both a precaution and a legal necessity. They prevent someone from inserting additional language into blank spaces in the document after you have signed it. If you print an exported document (see "Exporting Your Document to a Text File," below), make sure that any hash marks in the version you print match those in the version displayed in Print Preview.

Revising Your Document

As you are reading your document, you may find information that you want to change. If so, you need to return to the document interview and provide new answers. (To find out how to change the *appearance* of your document—fonts, page margins and so on—see "Changing How Your Document Looks," below.)

Revising a Document That Uses a Checklist

Use the checklist to go directly to the part of the document interview containing the information you need to change. (To find out more about checklists, see "Using Checklists for Interview Management" in Part 3.)

To return to the appropriate part of your document interview and make changes:

1. Go to the "Congratulations" screen by clicking **Close Preview** or **Back** in Print Preview. (If you're not in Print Preview, see "Getting to the 'Congratulations' Screen," above.)
2. Click **Change Answers** to get to the checklist for your document.
3. Double-click the name of the interview part you need to revise (or select it and click **Next**).

4. Click through the screens in that part of the interview and review the information you previously entered, making changes as needed. When you've made it through all the screens, you'll return to the checklist.

5. If needed, repeat steps 3 and 4 for any other interview parts you need to revise.

6. Double-click **Preview and Print** on the checklist (or select it and click **Next**) to return to the "Congratulations" screen.

After you've made your changes, review your document once again in Print Preview before you print it.

Changing How Your Document Looks

Most of the time, you won't need to change the default formatting for your documents. However, if you do need to make formatting changes—changes to fonts, margins, spacing and so on—you can do so.

There are two places in Quicken WillMaker where you can reformat documents:

- The **Print Options** dialog box lets you change fonts and adjust page margins, line spacing and footer format.
- The **Print** dialog box lets you add a watermark ("Draft" or "Duplicate") to the document you are printing.

Both of these dialog boxes also let you specify basic printer setup options, including some that affect the look of your document: page orientation (portrait or landscape) and image quality.

To find out more about accessing these dialog boxes to make formatting adjustments, see below.

TIP

Restoring default format settings. If you decide to experiment with formatting adjustments, keep in mind that you can restore the default print-option settings at any time by choosing **File > Print Options**, then clicking **Use defaults**.

Adjusting Fonts, Footers, Margins and Spacing

To make adjustments to fonts, footers, margins and line spacing:

1. Choose **File > Print Options** (or click **Print Options** if you're in Print Preview). The **Print Options** dialog box opens.
2. Modify the option settings in the dialog box to make the changes you want. For more information about changing specific settings, see their descriptions below.
3. Click **OK**.

When you return to the displayed document, your changes will be reflected.

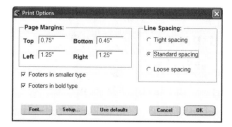

The **Print Options** dialog box includes the following elements:

Page Margins

These margins are measured in inches. To fit more text on each page, decrease the margin size by typing in smaller margin measurements.

Line Spacing

These options let you control how tightly spaced the text will be on the printed document. To fit more text on a page, select **Tight spacing**.

Footers in smaller type

When this option is checked, the type size of the footers at the bottom of each printed page will be smaller than that of the document text.

Footers in bold type

When this option is checked, the footers at the bottom of each printed page will appear in bold type.

Font...

Click this button to change the font, or its size, in a Windows **Font** dialog box.

Setup...

Click this button to change the printer, paper or network properties in a Windows **Print Setup** dialog box. (You can also specify printer and paper properties in the dialog box that appears when you choose **File > Print.**)

Use defaults

Click this button to restore all options specified in the **Print Options** dialog box to their default values.

Adding a Watermark to Identify a Draft or Duplicate Copy

If the copy you're printing is a draft or duplicate, we recommend adding a watermark to identify it as such, so it won't be confused with a final, signable document.

To add a watermark to your document, follow the steps in "Printing Your Document," below. When the **Print** dialog box appears, select **Draft** or **Duplicate** in the **Watermark** box (in the lower left corner) before clicking **OK**.

> CAUTION
> **Don't sign draft and duplicate copies.** To avoid confusion, sign only the final version of your document, making sure it does not have a draft or duplicate watermark.

Printing Your Document

To print your completed document:

1. Go to the "Congratulations" screen (see "Getting to the 'Congratulations' Screen," above), if you aren't already there.

2. Click **Preview and Print** to open the document preview.

3. You'll see a dialog box asking which specific documents in the document set you would like to display. If you don't want to print all of them, uncheck the ones you don't want before clicking **OK** (but be sure to include all of them when you print out the version you intend to sign and make legal).

4. Click **Print** (or choose **File > Print**) to open the **Print** dialog box.

5. Adjust the printing options available in the dialog box if necessary. If you are adding a watermark, see "Adding a Watermark to Identify a Draft or Duplicate Copy," above. If you are specifying page ranges and including signing instructions in your printout, see the cautionary note below.

6. Click **OK**.

> **CAUTION**
>
> **Page range counts may include instructions.** When you print your document, signing instructions are included unless you click **No** under **Print signing instructions** (found in the bottom right-hand corner of the **Print** dialog box). When included, these instructions print before the document.
>
> If you enter page numbers in the **From:** and **To:** boxes of the **Print range** section of the **Print** dialog box without turning off the option to print signing instructions, keep in mind that Quicken WillMaker counts from the first page actually printed, which is the first instruction page (some documents have more than one instruction page). Be sure to factor these extra pages in when you are specifying the range of pages you want to print.

If you're curious about slight differences between the printed version and the version you saw in Print Preview—or if you'd like to learn more about the hash marks ("/////") that print at the end of some pages—see "Reviewing Your Document in Print Preview," above.

Exporting Your Document to a Text File

It's easy to export a document to a text file. You may need to do this if:

- you are experiencing problems printing your document from Quicken WillMaker, or
- you need to email a copy of your document to someone who doesn't own a copy of Quicken WillMaker.

However, we strongly advise against exporting your document to another program for the purpose of editing document language. Editing your exported document can create significant problems, as noted below. Don't forget that Quicken WillMaker offers a substantial range of formatting options (see "Changing How Your Document Looks," above) for fine-tuning your document's appearance.

> **CAUTION**
>
> **Don't edit the language of your exported document.** Making changes to the language of a Quicken WillMaker document can create confusion, contradictions and legal problems that you may not be aware of. If you have questions about the language in a document, or if you would like to change its language, take the document to an experienced estate planning attorney and get advice on how to accomplish your goals.

The one type of edit that may be necessary is adjusting the hash marks ("////"), headers and footers to ensure the version you print matches the version displayed in Print Preview.

To export your document:

1. Go to the "Congratulations" screen (see "Getting to the 'Congratulations' Screen," above), if you aren't already there.
2. Click **Preview and Print** to open the document preview.
3. You'll see a dialog box asking which specific documents in the document set you would like to display. If you don't want to export all of the documents, uncheck the ones you don't want before clicking **OK** (but be sure to include all of them when you export a version you intend to sign and make legal).
4. Click the **Export** icon (or choose **File > Export Document**). After you see a warning message and click **Continue**, you'll see the **Export Document** dialog box.

5. Type a unique name for the file in the **File name** box. (If you don't use a unique name, any other file you have previously created with the same name will be erased.)

6. Select a file type—either Rich Text Format (.rtf) or plain text (.txt)—from the **Save as type** drop-down menu. If your word processor can read Rich Text Format, select this option, which preserves more formatting.

7. Click **Save**.

8. You'll then see a dialog box asking whether you'd like to view the exported file. Click **Yes** to open the file in your default word processor. If you click **No**, you'll need to use My Computer or Windows Explorer to locate your exported file so you can open it.

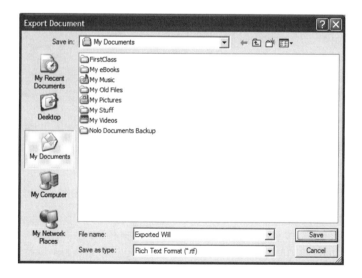

To view or print the exported document, you'll have to open it with a word processing or text editing program—preferably Microsoft Word or Word Viewer (see below). Be sure to read the instructions in the exported file about how to place the proper headers and footers to correctly format your document—then delete these instructions before printing out your document.

> **TIP**
>
> **Open your exported .rtf file in Microsoft Word or Word Viewer.** If you export your document in .rtf (Rich Text Format) and open it in a program other than Microsoft Word or Word Viewer, your documents may have problems (such as missing formatting, incorrect page numbering or missing signature lines) that you'll need to correct manually. If you don't have Word, you can download Word Viewer for free from Microsoft.com's Download Center.

Managing Your Documents in Portfolios

I n Quicken WillMaker, a "portfolio" is the file where your documents and Contact List are saved. Portfolios have the extension ".pfls."

If you simply want to create a will for yourself with Quicken WillMaker, you may not ever need to know about portfolios. The Document List (see Part 3) offers plenty of basic document-management capabilities: You can see what documents you've created, and you can open them to revise or print. Plus, the program automatically saves your documents and makes backup copies on your computer.

However, if you need to perform more complex document-management tasks, such as moving your documents to other locations or protecting them with passwords, you need to learn a bit about portfolios.

This part of the Users' Manual introduces portfolios and describes how to create and save portfolios, password-protect them and back them up.

Understanding Portfolios

A Quicken WillMaker portfolio stores your documents, along with your Contact List information.

This "one file" approach offers important advantages:

- You can easily share contact information (and changes in that information) among documents.
- It helps prevent confusion that might arise from keeping your documents in multiple places.

Portfolios can be a bit confusing if you're used to programs that save each document in a separate file. Remember: With Quicken WillMaker, you can create many documents, but they're all stored in one portfolio.

Creating a Portfolio

Quicken WillMaker uses the name you enter in the introduction to create a portfolio file for you.

If you decide to create additional portfolios, you can return to the "Enter Your Name" screen with the simple menu command described below. We recommend that each person in your family who uses Quicken WillMaker create a separate portfolio file, to avoid confusion about whose documents are in what file. (To find out how to share contact information among users, see Part 6.)

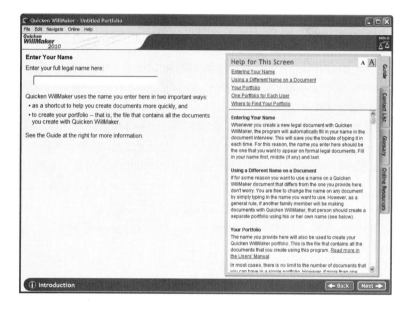

To create a portfolio:

1. Go to the "Enter Your Name" screen, if you're not already there, by choosing **File > New Portfolio**.

2. Type your name (or, if the portfolio is for someone else, have that person type his or her name) in the text entry box.

3. Click **Next** or press ENTER.

4. When you next see the **Save File** dialog box (either now or later, depending on your saving preferences), check that the default file name and save location are what you want, then click **Save**. For more information about saving portfolios, see "Saving Your Portfolio," below.

Unless you specify otherwise, the program names the portfolio "Portfolio of *[name you entered]*.pfls" and saves it to your **My Documents** (Windows XP) or **Documents** (Windows Vista) folder. It also creates an identical backup portfolio to use if a problem occurs with the original file. (To find out more about backup portfolios, see "Opening a Backup Portfolio," below.)

Opening a Portfolio

If there are multiple portfolios on your computer, it's important to pay attention to which one you have open at any given time—and to know how to switch among them.

Each time you start Quicken WillMaker, the program automatically opens the portfolio that was open the last time you quit the program. You can't have more than one portfolio open at a time; so if you open another portfolio, the program automatically closes the one that was open.

How you open a portfolio depends on whether you've used it recently or not.

Opening a Recently Used Portfolio

To open a portfolio you used recently:

1. Choose **File > Recent Files** to see a submenu of recently used portfolios.
2. Click the name of the portfolio you want to use.

The program opens the portfolio you selected.

Saving Your Portfolio

If the **Automatically save changes** feature is turned on in the program preferences, the program automatically saves data to the currently open portfolio as you move from one interview screen to the next. If this feature is turned off, you'll need to save data manually.

To find out how to save data manually and how to change your program preferences, see "Saving Your Data" in Part 3.

Protecting Your Portfolio With a Password

If your computer has multiple users, you may want to ensure the privacy of your Quicken WillMaker documents by assigning your portfolio a password. Once you've done so, no one can unlock your portfolio without knowing the password.

This section of the manual describes how to lock and unlock a portfolio, as well as how to change a portfolio's password.

Locking a Portfolio

To lock the currently open portfolio:

1. Choose **File > Lock Portfolio** to open the **New Password** dialog box.

2. Enter the password you want to use (the program asks you to do this twice to make sure you typed it correctly), along with a hint to help you remember the password. *Note that your password is case sensitive*, so you'll need to remember exactly how you entered it.

3. Click **OK** for this dialog box and the subsequent one, which tells you your portfolio has been locked.

The next time you try to open the portfolio, the program will display a **Portfolio Locked** dialog box. You'll need to enter the password and click **OK** to open the file.

> **TIP**
> **Take care when choosing your hint.** Once your portfolio is locked, you can't open it without first entering the correct password. While the program does let you unlock a portfolio or change its password (see below), you can't do so unless the portfolio is already open. So, be careful when you choose your password and make your hint as useful as possible. For example, instead of just saying "name of favorite horse" for your hint, say "name of favorite horse (no caps or abbreviations)," so you'll remember you spelled it "mistered" instead of, say, "MrEd."

Unlocking a Portfolio

To unlock the currently open portfolio:
- Choose **File > Unlock Portfolio**.

A dialog box informs you that your portfolio has been unlocked.

Changing a Portfolio's Password

To change the password assigned to the currently open portfolio:

1. Choose **File > Change Portfolio Password** to open the **New Password** dialog box.
2. Enter the new password you want to use, along with a hint to help you remember the password.
3. Click **OK** for this dialog box and the next one that displays, which tells you your portfolio has been locked.

Opening a Backup Portfolio

Whenever Quicken WillMaker creates a portfolio, it also creates an identical backup copy of it. Each time the program saves data to your portfolio, it also saves the same data to your backup portfolio. This backup can come in handy if a problem ever occurs with your original file.

Unless you specify otherwise, Quicken WillMaker stores backup portfolios in the **Nolo Documents Backup** subfolder of your **My Documents** (Windows XP) or **Documents** (Windows Vista) folder.

To protect you from accidentally overwriting your backup portfolios, Quicken WillMaker doesn't let you open portfolios stored in the **Nolo Documents Backup** folder. If you encounter a problem with a portfolio and need to open its backup portfolio, you must first copy the backup portfolio and paste this copy into another location outside of the backup folder.

To open a backup portfolio:

1. In Windows, locate the **Nolo Documents Backup** folder. If it isn't in your **My Documents** (Windows XP) or **Documents** (Windows Vista) folder, use the Windows Search feature to find it.

2. Open the **Nolo Documents Backup** folder and locate the backup portfolio you want to open.

3. Copy the backup portfolio and paste it into a different folder or onto the desktop, using your favorite Windows method for copying and pasting files. Remember the name and location of this copied portfolio.

4. In Quicken WillMaker, choose **File > Open Portfolio.**

5. Locate the file you want to open. In most cases, it will be in your **My Documents** (Windows XP) or **Documents** (Windows Vista) folder. If you can't find it, use the Windows Search feature (**Start > Search**) to search for all files on your computer with a ".pfls" file extension.

6. Click **Open**.

Managing Your Contact Information

When you enter information about people and organizations in document interviews, Quicken WillMaker automatically adds it to your Contact List. This saves you from having to enter it again in other documents. The Contact List is stored in your portfolio with the documents you create.

While the program creates and maintains your Contact List in the background, you can also work directly with your Contact List. For example, changing a name in the Contact List changes that name in all the documents that contain it. You can also access your Contact List for other contact-management purposes, such as printing information about your contacts or importing contact information from another portfolio.

This part of the Users' Manual discusses how to:

- access your Contact List
- add names to your Contact List
- revise contact information you've already entered
- delete names from your Contact List
- locate names in your documents
- import contacts from another portfolio, and
- print your Contact List.

Accessing Your Contact List

Quicken WillMaker provides two ways for you to access your Contact List:

- The onscreen Guide lets you view or edit Contact List entries during an interview.
- The **Manage Contact List** dialog box provides a wider range of Contact List management options.

For tasks other than editing previously entered contact information during an interview, use the second option.

Accessing Contact List Entries From the Guide

If you are in the middle of an interview, the onscreen Guide offers a handy way for you to view or edit the information in your Contact List.

To access the Contact List entries from the Guide:

- Click the **Contact List** tab on the right-hand edge of the Guide.

A list of the names in your Contact List appears in the Guide. Click any name to view or edit its associated contact information (address, phone number and so on).

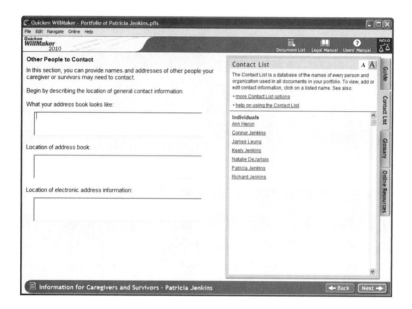

Accessing Contact List Management Options

To access a full range of options for managing your Contact List:

- Choose **Edit > Manage Contact List**.

The **Manage Contact List** dialog box appears, with buttons for adding, deleting, revising, importing and printing contact information and for locating documents that contain specific names. (For more information on these tasks, see below.)

When you're done performing the tasks available in this dialog box, click **Done**.

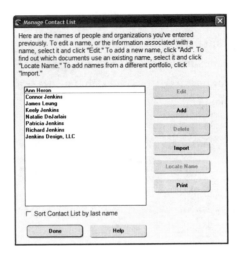

Adding Names to Your Contact List

Whenever you type a name into a text box during a document interview and go to the next interview screen, Quicken WillMaker checks to make sure the name isn't already in your Contact List, then adds it. If you like, you can also enter names directly into the Contact List.

To add the name of a person or organization directly into your Contact List:

1. Choose **Edit > Manage Contact List** to display the **Manage Contact List** dialog box, if it's not already displayed.
2. Click **Add** to display the **Name Information** dialog box.
3. Type the name in the **Name** text-entry box.
4. Click the appropriate radio button to identify whether you have named a male, a female or an organization.
5. Type in any additional information in the appropriate areas of the **Additional Information** box.
6. Click **OK** to return to the **Manage Contact List** dialog box.

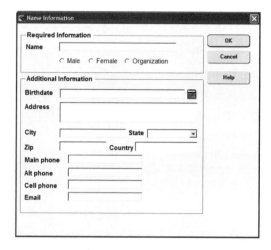

Revising Contact Information

To revise the information for a particular name in your contact list, you first need to access the **Name Information** dialog box for that contact name. You can access this dialog box in either of two ways; which method you use depends on how you have accessed your Contact List (see "Accessing Your Contact List," above):

- If you clicked the **Contact List** tab in the Guide, click the contact's name from the list showing in the Guide.
- If you are using the **Manage Contact List** dialog box, select the contact's name, then click **Edit**.

Once the **Name Information** box is showing, make any changes you want to make, then click the **OK** button.

> **TIP**
>
> **Revising the spelling of a contact name.** To revise the spelling of a contact name, click **Edit Name**. Clicking this button brings up the **Edit Name** dialog box, which tells you that any change you make in the name will ripple through all your documents. Type in your correction, then click **OK**.

Deleting Names From Your Contact List

If a name is not used in any of the Quicken WillMaker documents in your portfolio, you can delete it from the Contact List as follows:

1. Choose **Edit > Manage Contact List** to display the **Manage Contact List** dialog box, if it's not already displayed.

2. Select the name you want to delete.

3. Click **Delete.**

TIP

Use the Locate Names button to find names you want to delete. If you try to delete a name that is used in one or more of your documents, you'll see a dialog box telling you that you can't delete the name from your Contact List and giving you a list of the documents in which the name appears. You can use the **Locate Name** button to find out where the name appears. (See "Locating Names in Your Documents," just below.) You can then revise the documents to remove the name. When the name is no longer used in any documents, you'll be able to delete the name from the Contact List. (For information about revising documents, see "Revising Your Document" in Part 4.)

Locating Names in Your Documents

To find out which of the documents in your portfolio contain a particular name:

1. Choose **Edit > Manage Contact List** to display the **Manage Contact List** dialog box, if it's not already displayed.

2. Select the name you want to locate.

3. Click **Locate Name** to display the **Documents Containing This Name** dialog box.

4. When you have noted which documents contain the name in question (you may want to print out or write down the document names), click **OK.**

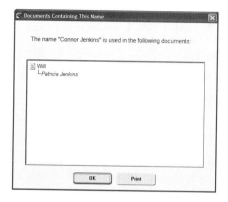

Importing Contacts From Other Contact Lists

If your family members have created separate portfolios (see "Creating a Portfolio" in Part 5), you can share contact information for contacts you have in common. You do this by importing Contact List data from one portfolio into another.

To import Contact List information from another portfolio into the one currently open:

1. Choose **Edit > Manage Contact List** to display the **Manage Contact List** dialog box, if it's not already displayed.
2. Click **Import** to open the **Select the file you want to import names from:** dialog box.
3. Locate and select the Quicken WillMaker portfolio from which you want to import Contact List information. (If you're having trouble finding it, use the Windows Search feature (**Start > Search**) to search for all files on your computer with a ".pfl" file extension.)
4. Click **Open**.
5. Read the dialog box that tells you how many names you've imported, then click **OK**.

When you import names, only those names *not* already in your portfolio are added.

Printing Your Contact List

To print the information in your Contact List:

1. Choose **Edit > Manage Contact List** to display the **Manage Contact List** dialog box, if it's not already displayed.

2. Click **Print** to open the **Print** dialog box.

3. Adjust the printing options available in the dialog box if necessary, then click **OK**.

Your contact information is printed with people listed first, then organizations. Names are in alphabetical order by first name of person or first word of organization name—unless you checked the **Sort Contact List by last name** box in the **Manage Contact List** dialog box. If you checked this box, the list is printed in alphabetical order by last name of person or last word of organization name.

Getting Help

Any time you have a question about how to do something with Quicken WillMaker, help is close at hand. The key to answering your question as quickly as possible is knowing which help resource to consult.

The table below shows which help resource to use for the type of help you need. It also refers you to specific sections of Part 7 that will help you use these resources.

Using the Onscreen Guide

The Guide that you see on the right-hand side of each interview screen in Quicken WillMaker helps you answer the specific questions on that screen. The text includes both legal and practical information related to the current screen, plus links to related topics in the electronic manuals and on the Internet. In addition, the tabs along the right edge of the Guide provide quick access to your Contact List information, a glossary of legal terms and a page with links to online resources.

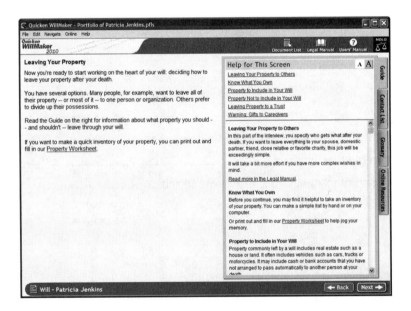

What You Need	Help Resource to Consult	Section(s) of Part 7 to Read
Help understanding how to complete the current interview question or screen	The onscreen Guide (right-hand side of screen)	"Using the Onscreen Guide"
In-depth legal information to help you decide how to answer an interview question	The Legal Manual (printed or electronic version)	"Using the Electronic Manuals"
Definitions of legal terms	The Glossary in the onscreen Guide or Nolo's online glossary	"Looking Up Definitions of Legal Terms" and "Accessing Online Resources"
Help locating a lawyer	Nolo's online Lawyer Directory	"Accessing Online Resources"
Practical advice about how to use the program	This Users' Manual (printed or electronic version)	"Using the Electronic Manuals," plus other applicable sections of this manual (consult the Index or the Table of Contents)
Help fixing a problem you're having with the program	This Users' Manual (printed or electronic version)	"Dealing With Problems"
Additional assistance for a problem you haven't been able to solve using the manual	Nolo Technical Support	"Contacting Nolo Technical Support and Customer Service"

You don't need to do anything to access the Guide; it automatically appears on each interview screen. As you move to a new screen, the Guide text changes to provide specific help for that screen.

This section provides some tips for using the Guide and describes how to:

- change the Guide's font size
- copy text from the Guide, and
- print help topics from the Guide.

Tips for Finding Information in the Guide

Sometimes, the "Help for This Screen" displayed for a particular page is extensive. To help you quickly find what you're looking for, here are some tips:

- Click the topic names at the top of the Guide, directly under "Help for This Screen," to go directly to those topics instead of having to scroll through the text.
- For more in-depth information on a topic than is shown in the Guide, click "Read more" links when they appear. These links open a relevant part of one of the electronic manuals in a separate window. (For more information about these manuals, see "Using the Electronic Manuals," below.)
- Web links, which are underlined and preceded by a "globe" icon 🌐 open a separate browser window in which you can view a related website. When you've looked at the website, you can return to Quicken WillMaker by closing or minimizing your browser, using your Windows taskbar or pressing ALT+TAB.
- If you need access to online resources or help with terminology, click the **Online Resources** or **Glossary** tab. (See "Accessing Online Resources" and "Looking Up Definitions of Legal Terms," below.)

Changing the Guide's Font Size

The two **A** icons in the title bar at the top of each Guide page let you change the font size of the text in the Guide:

| Help for This Screen | A A |

- To show the text in a larger font size, click the icon with the larger **A**.
- To return the text to the smaller font size, click the icon with the smaller **A**.

The change of font size will take effect immediately.

Copying Text From the Guide

To copy text from the Guide and paste it into an email or word processing document:

1. Select the text you want to copy.
2. Copy it to your clipboard by pressing CTRL+C.
3. Click where you want to insert the text, then paste it there by pressing CTRL+V.

Printing Help Topics From the Guide

To print the Guide text for the screen you're currently viewing:

1. Choose **File > Print Guide Topic** to open the standard **Print** dialog box.
2. Make any changes you want to the print options, then click **OK**.

Using the Electronic Manuals

Quicken WillMaker's help system includes electronic versions of the program's two manuals:

- this Users' Manual, which provides practical advice to help you use the program, and
- the Legal Manual, which contains in-depth legal information written in plain English to help you answer the program's interview questions knowledgeably.

This section describes how to:

- access the electronic manuals
- navigate a manual's contents
- print a topic from a manual
- print a chapter or entire manual, and
- view a PDF version of the Users' Manual.

Accessing the Electronic Manuals

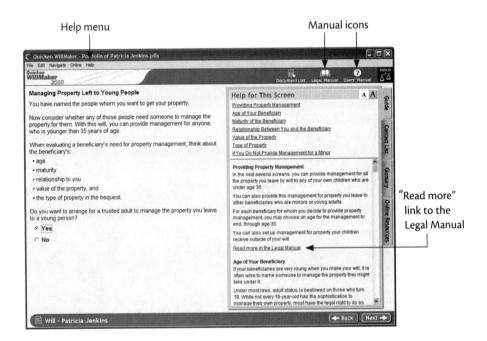

You can access an electronic manual in any of the following three ways:

- from the **Help** menu (choose **Help > Quicken WillMaker Users' Manual** or **Help > Quicken WillMaker Legal Manual**)

- by clicking the manual's icon on the navigation bar above the Guide, or
- by clicking a "Read more" link in the Guide text.

Navigating a Manual's Contents

When you open one of the manuals as described above, it appears in its own window on top of the main Quicken WillMaker program window. If you click the **Show** button on the button bar at the top of the window, the window expands to include a navigation pane along the left side, offering you additional navigation options. The expanded manual window includes three main areas (described in detail below):

- the topic pane
- the button bar, and
- the navigation pane.

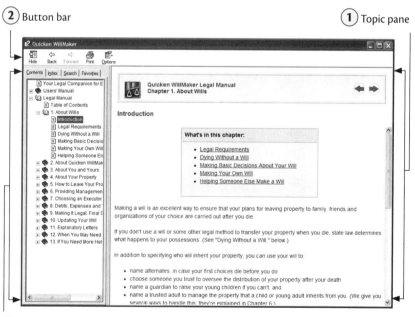

② Button bar   ① Topic pane

③ Navigation pane

① Topic Pane

The topic pane displays the text of the manual. The area at the top tells you which manual, chapter and topic you're viewing.

At the top (upper right corner) and bottom of each topic are arrows that link to:

- the *previous* topic in the current chapter (or the last topic in the previous chapter, if you're at the beginning of a chapter), and
- the *next* topic in the current chapter (or the first topic in the next chapter, if you're at the end of a chapter).

Many topics include underlined links to related topics and websites. You can click on them to go to related manual sections or websites; the latter open in a separate browser window.

② Button Bar

The button bar at the top of the manual window contains the following buttons:

- **Show/Hide.** Displays (or hides) the navigation pane, which provides access to additional navigational options. (See "Navigation Pane," below.)
- **Back.** Takes you through the manual topics you've already reviewed, in reverse order. (This button is similar to the backward arrow in your Web browser.)
- **Forward.** If you've used the **Back** button to return to a previously viewed topic, you can use this button to move to the topic you were viewing when you clicked the **Back** button. (This button is similar to the forward arrow in your Web browser.)
- **Print.** Opens a dialog box that gives you the option of printing sections of the manual. (See "Printing a Topic From a Manual" and "Printing a Chapter or Entire Manual," below.)

- **Options.** Opens a menu list that contains items for all the buttons listed above (for easy keyboard access to these options), plus a few other options. The **Internet Options** command opens Internet Explorer's **Internet Options** dialog box. The **Search Highlight On/ Off** command turns highlighting for search terms on or off.

③ **Navigation Pane**

The navigation pane doesn't appear when you first open the manual window; you need to click **Show** (in the button bar) to see it. The navigation pane has four tabs:

- **Contents.** Displays the manual's table of contents. You can use the +/– icons next to the manual and chapter titles to show or hide the chapter names and topics. If you have opted to locate the currently displayed topic, the topic name is highlighted in the table of contents. To display a topic listed in the table of contents in the topic pane, double-click the topic name.
- **Index.** Displays the manual's index. To display a topic listed in the index in the topic pane, double-click the topic name in the index (or select it and click the **Display** button at the bottom of the pane).
- **Search.** Displays a search tool that provides a full-text search of every page in both manuals. Type the words you want to search for in the text-entry box, then click the **List Topics** button. The search tool lists all topics that contain the words you searched for. Topic names are prefaced to identify whether the information is in the Legal Manual ("LEGAL"), the Users' Manual ("USER"), a sample document ("SAMPLE") or a help topic accessible from a dialog box ("HELP"). To display a topic in the topic pane, double-click its name (or select its name and click the **Display** button near the top of the pane).
- **Favorites.** Displays a list (initially blank) of your favorite topics. You can (when the topic is showing in the topic pane) remove and display topics by using the buttons below the Favorites list.

To hide the navigation pane, click the **Hide** button on the button bar.

Printing a Topic From a Manual

To print the text of the manual topic you're currently viewing:

1. Click **Print** on the window's button bar. What happens next depends on whether the navigation pane is hidden or showing; if it's hidden, the **Print** dialog box appears immediately, so you can skip the next step.
2. If the navigation pane is showing, you'll see the **Print Topics** dialog box; select the option **Print the selected topic** and click **OK** to open the **Print** dialog box.
3. In the **Print** dialog box, make any changes you want to the print options, then click **Print**.

Printing a Chapter or Entire Manual

To print a chapter of the Users' Manual or Legal Manual after you have opened its electronic version:

1. Display the **Contents** tab in the window's navigation pane. (See "Navigating a Manual's Contents," above.)
2. Select the name of the manual or chapter you want to print by clicking it. (If only the manual's names are showing and you want to print a chapter, click the + icon next to the manual's name to display the chapter titles.)
3. Click **Print** on the window's button bar to open the **Print Topics** dialog box.
4. Select the option **Print the selected heading and all subtopics**.
5. Click **OK** to open the **Print** dialog box.
6. Make any changes you want to the print options, then click **Print**.

The method described above prints the manual's pages as they appear in the electronic version. If you are printing part of the Users' Manual and would prefer for the pages to appear as they do in the printed version, you can open the PDF version as described below and print from that version.

Viewing a PDF Version of the Users' Manual

The electronic version of the Users' Manual that you can access from the program is designed to work well on screen but lacks the illustrations and some of the formatting found in the printed version. So, we've also included a PDF version with the same formatting as the printed manual. You can view it if you have Adobe *Reader* version 5.0 or greater installed on your computer. (You can download Adobe *Reader* for free from www.adobe.com.)

To view the PDF version of the Users' Manual in Adobe *Reader*:

- From the Windows taskbar, choose **Start > Programs** (or **All Programs**) **> Quicken WillMaker 2010 > Users' Manual**.

Looking Up Definitions of Legal Terms

When you're answering interview questions, you may encounter a legal or estate planning term you're not familiar with. To find out what the term means, you can look up its definition in the program's glossary or consult Nolo's online glossary (see "Accessing Online Resources," below).

To look up the definition of a term in the program's glossary:

1. Click the **Glossary** tab on the right-hand edge of the Guide to open the glossary. At the top of the glossary, you'll see all the letters of the alphabet. Directly below are the glossary terms in alphabetical order.
2. At the top of the glossary, click the letter that begins the word you want to learn about. You'll then see a list of all glossary terms that begin with that letter.
3. Find the term you're interested in, scrolling if necessary to see more of the list, and click it to see its definition.

Many of the terms used in the definitions are underlined, indicating that those terms are also defined in the glossary. To see the definition of an underlined term, click on it.

Accessing Online Resources

Nolo provides many online resources that complement the help features available within Quicken WillMaker. These resources include a directory of lawyers in specific geographical areas, a glossary defining hundreds of legal terms and much more.

You can access Nolo's online resources in either of the following two ways:

- by clicking the **Online Resources** tab on the right-hand edge of the Guide and then clicking an underlined link to the specific resource you want, or
- by choosing **Online > Nolo on the Web**.

In either case, a Web page opens in a separate browser window.

Dealing With Problems

If you encounter a technical difficulty while running the program, this manual is the first resource you should consult. Which section you should read depends on the type of problem you're experiencing:

- If you're having trouble installing Quicken WillMaker because the setup program doesn't launch, see "Jump-Starting the Setup Program," below.
- If you're having trouble printing from the program, see "Correcting Printing Problems," below.
- If you're having trouble with the program's Web Update feature (discussed in "Updating Your Version of the Program," in Part 2), see "Handling Web Update Problems," below.
- If you're encountering an error message, consult the table in Appendix C. This table explains the meaning of each error message and describes what to do if you encounter it.

If none of the above situations apply and you can't find a section of this manual that helps with your problem, look in the **Troubleshooting** file in your **Quicken WillMaker 2010** program folder (see "Checking Out the Program Folder" in Part 2); you may find advice relevant to your problem.

If none of the above suggestions help, contact Nolo Technical Support. (See "Contacting Nolo Technical Support and Customer Service," below.)

Jump-Starting the Setup Program

When you insert the Quicken WillMaker Installation CD into your CD-ROM drive, setup should launch automatically. If it doesn't, here's what to do:

1. Choose **Start > Run...** (Windows XP) or **Start > All Programs > Accessories > Run...** (Windows Vista).
2. Type **D:\AUTORUN** (you may have to substitute the letter of your CD-ROM drive for "D").
3. Click **OK**.

Correcting Printing Problems

If you're having a printing problem in Quicken WillMaker, try the following remedies:

- If you are having trouble getting your document to print, go to the **Print Setup** dialog box (**File > Print Setup**) and make sure the settings for your printer are correct, then click **OK** and try to print again.
- If you are not satisfied with the formatting of a printed document, go to the **Print Options** dialog box (**File > Print Options**) to make adjustments. For example, if you're getting a page with very little text and lots of hash marks ("/////"), try making the bottom margin larger (changing it from 0.45 inch to 0.6 inch will usually correct the problem). (For information about why hash marks are legally necessary, see "Reviewing Your Document in Print Preview" in Part 4.)

If neither of the above suggestions help, you can export your document and print it using your word processor (see "Exporting Your Document to a Text File" in Part 4)—and please contact Nolo Technical Support to report the problem, so we can investigate the problem and fix it, if necessary. (See "Contacting Nolo Technical Support and Customer Service," below.)

Handling Web Update Problems

If you encounter problems with the program's Web Update feature (see "Updating Your Version of the Program" in Part 2), check the table below. If any of the situations listed there apply to you, try the suggested remedy for your problem.

> CAUTION
> **Web Update isn't designed to work with proxy servers and other corporate VPN configurations.** If you are trying to update the program behind a corporate proxy server and getting various error messages, you won't be able to use Web Update. Web Update is designed for the home user with a basic firewall. Unfortunately, we can't support proxy servers and other corporate VPN (Virtual Private Network) security configurations.

If none of the above suggestions help, and you can't find relevant advice in the **Troubleshooting** file (see "Checking Out the Program Folder" under "Installing Quicken WillMaker" in Part 2), contact Nolo Technical Support (see below).

When contacting Nolo Technical Support about a Web Update problem, include the following details in addition to those normally required for other types of problems:

- the type of Internet connection you have (modem dial-up, DSL or other), and
- the name of your Internet service provider.

If you are:	Try this remedy for your problem:
A Windows XP user getting an error message because you don't have the administrator privileges required for installing program files ...	Switch to a user with administrator privileges or have your system's security settings changed. If necessary, contact your network administrator or read Windows documentation on changing security settings.
A Windows Vista user encountering a "User Access Control" dialog box when the update finishes ...	Click **Continue** in the dialog box or enter an administrator password as prompted.
Using a firewall or security application (see below for the case of Windows XP Service Pack 2) and receiving warnings ...	Add "f1.nolo.com" to the "trusted site" list. If you still can't complete the update after making this addition, you may need to turn off your firewall program while retrieving the update, then turn it back on.
A Windows XP Service Pack 2 user getting a Windows Security Alert asking whether you want to keep blocking or to unblock your Quicken WillMaker's Internet connection ...	Select **Unblock**. Once you have unblocked Quicken WillMaker, you should be able to download future Web Updates.

Contacting Nolo Technical Support and Customer Service

If you're encountering a problem that isn't addressed in this section of the manual or Appendix C, you may find an answer on Nolo's website. Nolo's Technical Support department posts FAQs with answers to common user questions and problems.

To find the FAQ page for this program, go to Nolo's Technical Support page at www.nolo.com/support/software_faq.cfm.

If you can't find a solution on the FAQ page, contact Nolo Technical Support directly.

Email address: support@nolo.com

Phone number: 510-549-4660

Phone hours: 9:00 a.m. to 5:00 p.m. Pacific time, Monday through Friday

When you call, try to be in front of the computer with which you are having the problem. Also, whether you are emailing or calling, be sure to have the information noted below on hand.

Information to Have on Hand

When you contact Nolo Technical Support about a problem, please include the following information in your email (or have it ready before you call):

- the version of Quicken WillMaker you're running, located at **Help > About Quicken WillMaker 2010**
- the point in the program where the problem occurred
- whether you can duplicate the problem
- the brand and model of computer you are using
- the brand and model of printer (if you are having trouble printing)
- the name of your Internet service provider and the type of Internet connection you have (if you are having a problem that involves connecting to the Internet)
- which version of which operating system your computer is running (for example, XP Home Service Pack 2), and
- the amount of RAM on your computer.

If you're not sure which model of computer you have, how much RAM it has or which version of the operating system it's running, see below.

Finding Information About Your Computer System

How you find information about your computer system depends on which operating system it's running.

Windows Vista:

- Choose **Start > Computer > System Properties**.

Windows XP:

1. Right click the **My Computer** icon on your desktop.
2. Select **Properties**.
3. Choose the tab that contains the information you need.

Menu Options

This section lists the commands available in each of the program's menus and describes what they do. To access any menu option:
1. Click the menu in Quicken WillMaker's menu bar.
2. Select the command.

If you prefer not using your mouse, just type the first letter in the menu name while pressing the ALT key, then type the letter underlined in the option name.

File Menu

New Portfolio

Use this command to create a new Quicken WillMaker portfolio.

Open Portfolio...

Use this command to open portfolios made with Quicken WillMaker 2010.

Save

Use this command to manually save your currently open portfolio. You do not need to use this command if **Automatically save changes** is on.

Save As...

Use this command to rename your portfolio and/or save it to another location on your computer.

Lock/Unlock Portfolio

Use this command to lock your portfolio and give it a password. If your portfolio is locked, no one can open it without first entering the password. If you want to unlock a portfolio you've locked, you'll first need to enter the password you assigned to it.

Change Portfolio Password

Use this command to change your password. This command is available only if you have previously locked your portfolio.

Print Options...

Use this command to change the formatting for your documents, including page margins, line spacing, font type and font size. We recommend keeping the default settings.

Print Setup...

Use this command to open the standard **Print Setup** dialog box for the currently chosen printer.

Print Guide Topic...

Use this command to print the Guide topic displayed in the current interview screen. If you don't see this command, click the **Guide** tab and then try opening the **File** menu.

Print Contact List...

Use this command to print the Contact List for the currently open portfolio. If you don't see this command, click the **Contact List** tab and then try opening the **File** menu.

Export Document...

Use this command to save your displayed document as a text file that you can view, edit or print with a word processor.

Recent Files

Use this command to open a recently used portfolio file (.pfl). This submenu lists up to five files.

Exit

Use this command to quit the Quicken WillMaker program.

Edit Menu

Undo

Use this command to undo the last typing or editing action you performed, provided you haven't left the screen on which the changes were made.

Cut

Use this command to remove selected text and add it to the Clipboard.

Copy

Use this command to copy selected text to the Clipboard, without removing it.

Paste

Use this command to insert text that you have previously cut or copied at the blinking cursor, or to replace selected text with text that you have previously cut or copied.

Delete

Use this command to delete selected text without adding it to the Clipboard. The selected text will not be saved.

Select All

Use this command to select all the text in the currently active text field.

Check Spelling

Use this command to check the spelling of text you typed in answering an interview question. Make sure your mouse cursor is inside the text box where you typed your answer before choosing **Edit > Check Spelling.**

Duplicate Document

Use this command to create a new document by duplicating one you've already created. To use this command, you must select the document you want to duplicate in the Document List.

Delete Document

Use this command to delete a document you've already created. To use this command, you must select the document you want to delete in the Document List.

Duplicate Will for Spouse/Domestic Partner

Use this command to make an identical will for your spouse or registered partner. For details on how couples can use this command to create identical wills, see "Creating an Identical Will for a Spouse or Partner" in Part 3.

Manage Contact List...

Use this command to add, modify or delete names in the Contact List, and to enter additional information about names previously entered.

Preferences...

Use this command to customize your version of Quicken WillMaker. You can use the **Preferences** command to specify the following:
- whether your data will be saved automatically or manually
- whether you want the program to fill in names automatically as you type them, based on entries in your Contact List
- whether you want the program to fill in related fields automatically after you enter a name
- whether you want the program to check for Web Updates automatically when you start it up
- whether you want to your entries automatically checked for spelling

- the font size of the Guide text, and
- the folder where your backup portfolios are stored.

Navigate Menu

Back

Use this command to go back to the previous screen.

Next

Use this command to move ahead to the next screen.

Go to Document List

Use this command to switch to a different Quicken WillMaker document interview. This command takes you to the Document List, from which you can start a new document or work on one you've already created.

Go to Introduction

Use this command to view the series of introductory screens you saw the first time you used the program.

Go to Interview

Use this command to start the interview of a document you've selected in the Document List, or to return to the interview if you're previewing the document in Print Preview.

Preview Document

Use this command to preview your completed document. You can use this command only after you have completed the document interview.

Online Menu

Web Update

Use this command to update your copy of Quicken WillMaker by downloading the latest updated files from the Web. Before you use this command, you must have a live Internet connection.

Online Registration

Use this command to register your copy of Quicken WillMaker. You'll need a Web browser and an Internet connection to use this command.

Nolo on the Web

Use this command to access Nolo's website at www.nolo.com. You'll need a Web browser and an Internet connection to use this command.

Help Menu

Quicken WillMaker Users' Manual

Use this command to display an electronic version of this manual.

Quicken WillMaker Legal Manual

Use this command to display an electronic version of the Legal Manual.

Product Support

Use this command if you need help with the program.

Suggestion Box

Use this command to see a Web page where you can give us feedback and suggestions about this program.

Keyboard Shortcuts

Use this command to see how to operate the program using a keyboard rather than a mouse.

About Quicken WillMaker 2010

Use this command to see information about which version of the program you're running, plus detailed information about all the program files you've installed.

Keyboard Shortcuts

This section lists keyboard shortcuts for performing the following types of actions:
- choosing options and exiting the program
- opening and saving portfolios
- displaying help resources
- navigating within and among screens, and
- navigating in a text-entry box.

To see this information when you're running the program, choose **Help > Keyboard Shortcuts**.

Choosing Options and Exiting the Program

Press ...	To ...
ENTER	Trigger the default button (as indicated by a thicker outline) or the selected button (if there is no default)—unless you are in a text-entry box that allows multiple entries, in which case pressing ENTER will start a new line of text.
ESC	Trigger the **Cancel, Close** or **No** button in a pop-up dialog box.
ALT+F4	Exit the program.

Opening and Saving Portfolios

Press ...	To ...
CTRL+O	Open an existing portfolio.
CTRL+S	Save the current portfolio when the **Automatically save changes** function is turned off.

Displaying Help Resources

Press ...	To ...
F1	Open the electronic version of the Users' Manual in a separate window.
CTRL+SHIFT+G	View the **Guide** tab at the right of an interview screen ("Help for This Screen").
CTRL+SHIFT+C	View the **Contact List** tab at the right of an interview screen.
CTRL+SHIFT+L	View the **Glossary** tab at the right of an interview screen.
CTRL+SHIFT+O	View the **Online Resources** tab at the right of an interview screen.

Navigating Within and Among Screens

Press ...	To ...
TAB	Move to the next part of the screen (such as a text box, list, button or group of option buttons).
SHIFT+TAB	Move to the previous part of the screen (such as a text box, list, button or group of option buttons).
DOWN ARROW	Highlight the next option button (in a group when one option button is selected), or the next item (in a selected list).
UP ARROW	Highlight the previous option button (in a group when one option button is selected), or the previous item (in a selected list).
ALT+RIGHT ARROW	Go to the next interview screen.
ALT+LEFT ARROW	Go back to the previous interview screen.

Navigating in a Text-Entry Box

Press ...	To ...
ENTER	Start a new line, if the box allows entry of multiple items.
LEFT ARROW	Move one character to left.
RIGHT ARROW	Move one character to right.
UP ARROW	Move one line up.
DOWN ARROW	Move one line down.
HOME	Move to the beginning of the line.
END	Move to the end of the line.
CTRL+HOME	Move to the beginning of the text-entry box.
CTRL+END	Move to the end of the entered text.
CTRL+LEFT ARROW	Move one word to left.
CTRL+RIGHT ARROW	Move one word to right.
CTRL+Z	Undo the most recent text editing action you have taken on the current screen, if the change has not yet been saved.
CTRL+X	Cut the selected text to the Clipboard.
CTRL+C	Copy the selected text to the Clipboard.
CTRL+V	Paste the contents of the Clipboard.
DELETE	Delete the selected text.
CTRL+A	Select all text in the current text-entry box.
CTRL+SHIFT+S	Check spelling of text in current text-entry box.

Error Messages

The table below describes what each error message means and what you should do if you encounter it. If the table entry for your error message suggests that you contact Nolo Technical Support, see "Contacting Nolo Technical Support and Customer Service" in Part 7 for contact information.

Error	What It Means	What You Should Do
[CD-ROM drive] is not accessible. The device is not ready	The CD you inserted is not being read.	Reinsert the CD. Wait ten seconds and double-click the CD-ROM drive icon. If that doesn't solve the problem, contact Nolo Technical Support.
[Name you're trying to edit information about]'s [name or gender] can't be changed. It's probably being used in a critical place in some document.	Editing this information could affect the legality of another document you've made.	Think about whether this change really needs to be made. If so, check other documents to see whether they require the same revision. If they do, you can make the revisions by creating new versions of the documents in question. Please read the appropriate sections of the Legal Manual before you start creating new document versions in this manner.

Error	What It Means	What You Should Do
A check on your interview answers revealed that some of your data is out of date or missing. Please review your answers by clicking "Change Answers" and reviewing the entire interview.	The program has determined that some of your data is out of date or missing.	Review all interview screens and make the necessary entries and revisions. If this problem continues, contact Nolo Technical Support.
An error exists in this Help file. Contact your application vendor for an updated Help file.	There's a problem opening the topic you selected in the program's Help system.	First, close the windows for any open Help files (including those from other programs), keeping Quicken WillMaker open. Then, repeat what you did that caused the error message. If the problem persists, contact Nolo Technical Support.
An error occurred: couldn't find the requested path name.	Quicken WillMaker couldn't find the path for a file it is trying to open.	Contact Nolo Technical Support.
An error occurred while assembling the document.	The resource files of the program might be damaged.	Reinstall the program and try again. If that doesn't work, contact Nolo Technical Support.
Internal error: attempt to overwrite existing file.	Quicken WillMaker is attempting to overwrite an existing file without permission.	Try to remember the steps you performed before the error appeared, then contact Nolo Technical Support.
Please select a part or option.	You clicked **Next** (or pressed ENTER) before you made a checklist selection.	Make a selection before clicking Next (or pressing ENTER).

Error	What It Means	What You Should Do
Quicken WillMaker cannot open that file (because it is read-only).	Quicken WillMaker was not allowed to open a file, either because it is in use or because it is read-only.	Make sure the file is located on your computer's hard drive in the My Documents folder, and check that neither the file nor the disk is locked.
Quicken WillMaker was not shut down properly the last time it was run. Please run Web Update to make sure your copy of the program is up-to-date. If this problem continues, contact Nolo Technical Support.	Either (1) a bug in Quicken WillMaker caused the program to crash the last time you used it, or (2) you turned off your computer while Quicken WillMaker was still running.	Run Web Update. If the problem was Quicken WillMaker, an update to fix the problem may be available. Also, make sure that you exit Quicken WillMaker before shutting down your computer. If this problem continues, contact Nolo Technical Support.
Sorry, a needed resource cannot be found.	The resource files of the program might be damaged.	Reinstall the program and try again. If that doesn't work, contact Nolo Technical Support.
Sorry, an internal data-module error occurred.	Something serious is wrong with the internal data structures.	Contact Nolo Technical Support.
Sorry, an internal error occurred.	Something serious is wrong with the program because of a disk error, a memory error or a bug.	Quit, restart the program, and attempt to repeat what you did. The problem may clear up on its own. If not, try reinstalling Quicken WillMaker. If that doesn't work, contact Nolo Technical Support.

Error	What It Means	What You Should Do
Sorry, but this version of Quicken WillMaker requires Internet Explorer version 6.0 or greater. Please install Internet Explorer 6.0 or later on your machine. Quicken WillMaker will now exit.	Your system does not meet the minimum requirements to run Quicken WillMaker.	If you don't run Internet Explorer, install it. If you run an old version, upgrade. You can download Internet Explorer free from Microsoft.com's Download Center.
Sorry, Quicken WillMaker can open only one portfolio at a time.	You attempted to open more than one Quicken WillMaker portfolio.	Open only one portfolio at a time.
Sorry, this file cannot be read by Quicken WillMaker.	You are trying to open a file that Quicken WillMaker doesn't recognize.	If you are sure the file you are attempting to use is a Quicken WillMaker portfolio file (that is, it has the extension ".pfl"), try a backup copy (see "Opening a Backup Portfolio" in Part 5). If that doesn't work, contact Nolo Technical Support.
Sorry, this file has been corrupted and cannot be read.	Your portfolio file has been seriously corrupted and cannot be read.	Use the backup portfolio with the same name.
Your document is not yet complete. Please complete the interview before printing your document.	The program has determined that it does not have all the information it needs to print your document.	Review all interview screens and enter any missing information. If you still can't print, contact Nolo Technical Support.

Index

NOLO® *Keep Up to Date*

1 Go to **Nolo.com/newsletters/index.html** to sign up for free newsletters and discounts on Nolo products.

- **Nolo Briefs.** Our monthly email newsletter with great deals and free information.

- **Nolo's Special Offer.** A monthly newsletter with the biggest Nolo discounts around.

- **BizBriefs.** Tips and discounts on Nolo products for business owners and managers.

- **Landlord's Quarterly.** Deals and free tips just for landlords and property managers, too.

2 Don't forget to check for updates at **Nolo.com.** Under "Products," find this book and click "Legal Updates."

Let Us Hear From You

3 Comments on this book? We want to hear 'em. Email us at feedback@nolo.com.

QWMB2010

NOLO® *Online Legal Forms*

Nolo offers a large library of legal solutions and forms, created by Nolo's in-house legal staff. These reliable documents can be prepared in minutes.

Online Legal Solutions

- **Incorporation.** Incorporate your business in any state.
- **LLC Formations.** Gain asset protection and pass-through tax status in any state.
- **Wills.** Nolo has helped people make over 2 million wills. Is it time to make or revise yours?
- **Living Trust (avoid probate).** Plan now to save your family the cost, delays, and hassle of probate.
- **Trademark.** Protect the name of your business or product.
- **Provisional Patent.** Preserve your rights under patent law and claim "patent pending" status.

Online Legal Forms

Nolo.com has hundreds of top quality legal forms available for download—bills of sale, promissory notes, nondisclosure agreements, LLC operating agreements, corporate minutes, commercial lease and sublease, motor vehicle bill of sale, consignment agreements and many, many more.

Review Your Documents

Many lawyers in Nolo's consumer-friendly lawyer directory will review Nolo documents for a very reasonable fee. Check their detailed profiles at **www.nolo.com/lawyers/index.html**.

NOLO® *Law for All*

Find an Estate Planning Attorney

- *Qualified lawyers*
- *In-depth profiles*
- *Respectful service*

When you want help with estate planning, you don't want just any lawyer—you want an expert in the field, who can provide up-to-the-minute advice to help you protect your loved ones. You need a lawyer who has the experience and knowledge to answer your questions about living trusts, wills, powers of attorney, estate taxes, probate, executors, life insurance and more.

Nolo's Lawyer Directory is unique because it provides an extensive profile of every lawyer. You'll learn about not only each lawyer's education, professional history, legal specialties, credentials and fees, but also about their philosophy of practicing law and how they like to work with clients. It's all crucial information when you're looking for someone to trust with an important personal or business matter.

All lawyers listed in Nolo's directory are in good standing with their state bar association. They all pledge to work diligently and respectfully with clients—communicating regularly, providing a written agreement about how legal matters will be handled, sending clear and detailed bills and more. And many directory lawyers will review Nolo documents, such as a will or living trust, for a fixed fee, to help you get the advice you need.

WWW.NOLO.COM

The attorneys shown above are fictitious. Any resemblance to an actual attorney is purely coincidental.